Small World Vegetable Gardening

Small World Vegetable Gardening

John E. Bryan

Drawings by Cathy Greene

101 Productions
San Francisco

Printed and bound in the United States of America.

Distributed to the book trade in the United States
by Charles Scribner's Sons, New York, and in Canada
by Van Nostrand Reinhold Ltd., Toronto.

Published by 101 Productions
834 Mission Street
San Francisco, California 94103

Library of Congress Cataloging in Publication Data

Bryan, John E   1931-
    Small world vegetable gardening.

    Includes index.
    1. Vegetable gardening.   I. Title.
SB321.B89   635   76-58364
ISBN 0-912238-79-8
ISBN 0-912238-78-X

Contents

The Ways of Vegetable Gardening 7

The Wherefores of Vegetable Gardening 11

Vegetable Culture 23

Specific Vegetables and Herbs 55

Container Gardening 159

Crop Rotation 177

    Vegetable Varieties 183

    First and Last Frost Dates 184

    Ordering Seeds by Mail 187

Index 189

The Whys of Vegetable Gardening

The pendulum is swinging away from the idea that earth was created for the benefit of man toward the belief that man is in charge of the earth and all its creatures as well as its plants. This burdens him with the awesome responsibility of not only caring for every one of his own kind, but also the ecological balance of all organisms with their environment. As he reaches out to the moon and other planets, his responsibilities multiply.

I would suggest that the pendulum is swinging too far, that man cannot be God's deputy, that he should strive for perfection, yet realize with great humility his well-developed brain cannot quickly solve universal problems.

For those who panic I highly recommend the calming and sobering experience of gardening in their own backyard, of dealing with a micro-ecology that can be unbelievably complex, of becoming intimately involved with plants for their economic and nutritional value, not merely decorative. After all, plants have provided the basic source of food for all animals since the beginning of time as well as clothing, shelter, fuel, medicines, tools, weapons, raw materials in addition to beauty.

Man takes great credit for developing strong stalks heavy with large kernels of grain from spindly wild grasses; giant blooms far more fragrant and colorful than necessary to attract birds, bees and butterflies to help with fertilization; plants that resist the elements and predators; trees, bushes and vegetables that produce food quicker and more prodigiously than their wild ancestors. Yet his efforts have not yet filled all the hungry mouths of today, let alone solving the problem of increasing numbers in the future. While home gardeners may contribute little to solving the overall problem, they *can* feel a sense of participation, especially if they learn a little about the history and life processes of plants.

It is humbling to realize that plants existed millions of years before animals—that evolving bacteria, yeasts, algae, mosses, pines and, finally, flowering plants and trees had to precede protozoa, insects, fishes, amphibians, reptiles, warmblooded animals and human-oids, because only plants can manufacture food from light, air, water and dissolved minerals alone. Plants can survive in environmental extremes where animals cannot—in the sea, in the ground, whether it be low swamps and deserts or high mountaintops, and in the air. The giant sequoia dwarfs both the dinosaur and the great blue whale, with a life cycle that spans thousands of years and hundreds of animal generations. Seeds can lie dormant, then spring to life given the proper temperature and moisture. Plants and animals complement each other, living on each other's products. The most important example is the plant's taking carbon dioxide from the air and exuding oxygen, the breath of life to animals. They feed on each other, for bacteria "devour" living animal tissue on occasion as surely as animals eat living plants. The pitcher plant and famous Venus's-flytrap supplement their air-water-mineral diet with high protein insects. Of the well over 300,000 plant species (not to mention the millions of varietals), some are credited with the capability of responding to music, speech and human feelings.

Some Cassandras proclaim evil man is destroying the earth by cutting trees, draining swamps, damming rivers and manufacturing unnatural molecules that pollute and destroy. I am the first to agree that in our zeal to make life better through science and technology we have gone down some primrose paths that have led into thorny brier thickets, and I would recommend more caution than we have sometimes shown in the past. But I would suggest that if we keep our wits about us, learn more about our environment, plants, other animals and ourselves and work steadily to preserve what is good as well as continue improving the quality of all life, we need not face the future with foreboding.

Dedicated gardeners are generally hard-working, humble and fascinated with the complexity of plants in general as well as each specie and individual plant. Gardeners consider themselves not to be gods, but rather partners of plants as they help the plants to reproduce and thrive under conditions which are often far from ideal—which, indeed, can present a real challenge. The rewards (and sometimes disappointments) can be great. Watching a bean being lifted out of the ground by its own root stem only to sprout in the air and sunshine with a shoot that little resembles the leaves and stalks that follow is great fun. Observing leaves and stalks growing rapidly as the plant twines itself around stakes, strings or its own stalks in a determined effort to reach the sky is like seeing a drama unfold. When blossoms change into succulent green pods, harvesting can be a treasure hunt. No matter how many are picked, there always seem to be a few, hidden and camouflaged, that are overlooked.

Digging and working the soil provides hours of healthy, outdoor exercise, along with terracing of slopes, building planter boxes, planting, weeding, watering. Vulnerable new sprouts, seedlings and transplants need to be protected and babied as they go through the trauma of birth or adjustment to a different environment. Insects, birds and other animals consider them great delicacies. Hardy weeds compete for nourishment and moisture. Vegetables can be most decorative if well tended, but of course the ultimate pleasure is in the eating, whether by the gardener nibbling as he harvests, by family and friends munching on raw hors d'oeuvre or by diners enjoying the special flavor of carefully cooked vegetables only hours away from the garden. Sometimes even a small garden can produce surpluses that can be preserved by early refrigeration, freezing or dry storage in a cool, dark area.

I consider vegetable growing on a small scale to be primarily a hobby, not a way of saving many dollars, because in most areas commercial growers and markets today efficiently provide a good variety of fresh, frozen or canned vegetables at reasonable prices. If you place a dollar value on your labor and add it to costs of seeds or small plants, tools, fertilizers, top soil, planter boxes, etc., you rarely can compete on the basis of economics. However, you *can* come out way ahead in other ways: in freshness, in choosing specially flavorful varieties too fragile for commercial growers to care for, harvest and ship; by growing vegetables and herbs the markets consider too esoteric to bother with; and by experimenting with out-of-season growing. I'm a firm believer in starting some plants indoors or in cold frames to get a jump on the season. I have reservations about vegetable growing indoors under lights or in greenhouses because of the high ratio of expense to yield, but it can be fun and quite a conversation piece. "Water growing," or hydroponics, because of its extreme complexity is beyond the scope of this book.

The micro-ecology of your own home can offer not only a challenge, but also new insight into what in recent years has become a matter of almost universal interest: the pattern of relations between organisms and their environment. As you become more intimately involved with vegetables, you may find the organisms more varied than you dreamed of, the environment far different from what you imagined it to be from the vantage point of a comfortable house. Even experienced farmers moving from acres to vest-pocket gardens often find a new challenge in deciding what to grow and how to produce greater yields per square foot.

10

The Wherefores of Vegetable Gardening

Plants we know as vegetables and herbs have played a vital role in man's existence since the dawn of history, many having been considered medicines centuries before becoming popular as foods. The origins of some are obscure, of others, better known. Their transport from region to region, from continent to continent, from the "Old" to the "New" World, or vice versa as restless explorers and colonizers roamed the earth is a matter of record.

Squashes, for example, were native to tropical America, but had found their way northward and southward into cooler climates long before 1492. Taken back to Europe, some became known as marrows in France and England. One rather obscure variety caught the fancy of Italian gardeners, who developed it into what became known as the zucchini, or Italian squash, which was reintroduced in the United States by 20th century immigrants. As recently as 25 years ago, many Americans of other ethnic groups had not even heard of it. Today this fast-growing, prolific squash is a favorite in most gardens and markets because of its versatility and flavor, raw or cooked. Other vegetables have had histories equally fascinating. Today, gardeners have literally a worldwide array to choose from.

But before getting into particular vegetables and their histories, before opening a seed catalogue with all its pretty, mouth-watering pictures and descriptions, before turning a shovelful of earth, it's well for a gardener to consider how plants live, grow and reproduce. Vegetables vary widely in form and growth patterns among themselves and are quite different in some ways from trees and shrubs, though being close relatives of many flowers. All flowering plants represent the highest form of plant life and share common life processes gardeners should be aware of.

11

PHOTOSYNTHESIS

If you're a bit vague about photosynthesis, take comfort from the fact that scientists are still exploring its mysteries. In the green parts of plants specialized cells are carrying on an amazing manufacturing process. They're taking six molecules of ground water and six molecules of carbon dioxide from the air and using light energy to produce one molecule of glucose, a simple sugar, and six molecules of oxygen. The glucose remains in the plant, while the oxygen is exuded into the air. Though math and chemistry are not primary subjects of this book, adding a few numbers to the above "recipe" results in exciting implications. The atomic weight of an atom of carbon "C" is 12, of hydrogen "H" 1, of oxygen "O" 16. Photosynthesis expressed as a formula is:

$$6 \ H_2O + 6 \ CO_2 \ \text{plus light yields} \ 1 \ C_6H_{12}O_6 + 6 \ O_2.$$

The atomic weight of the molecule of glucose produced is:

$$
\begin{array}{rl}
6 \ C @ 12 = & 72 \\
12 \ H @ \ 1 = & 12 \\
6 \ O @ 16 = & \underline{96} \\
\text{Total} & 180
\end{array}
$$

It's the glucose that is the plant's basic food. After conversion to more complex molecules it forms cellulose for cell walls and structural strength. Before 1450, horticulturists were convinced plants obtained their structural weight from the ground. At that time they concluded it was more likely that ground water was the major source. Two hundred years later doubts began to arise, but it was not until 1950 that sophisticated experiments conclusively proved that oxygen from the water passed into the air, with only the hydrogen left in the plant. This means that only 12 of the glucose's 180 weight, or 7 percent, comes from the ground water and that the other 93 percent comes from the air!

Of course, animals are not only interested in the glucose which they can eat, but in the six precious molecules of pure oxygen traded for six of carbon dioxide, almost like transmuting lead into gold. This process goes on under water as well as in the air with dissolved carbon dioxide being traded for dissolved oxygen for gills of fish. If a plant is deprived of light, water or air for any considerable time it feeds on its own stored food, the process is reversed and it turns yellow, then white, and finally dies. No wonder environmentalists feel so protective toward plants and their right to a place in the sun unclouded by dense smog.

The special plant cells that carry on photosynthesis are capable of absorbing carbon dioxide only after it's dissolved in moisture and exist not only in leaves, but also flowers, stems and sometimes roots. Their usual green color may be masked by other pigments. Their protoplasm comprises chlorophyll (from the Greek "green" and "leaf"), a complex organic compound containing nitrogen and magnesium in addition to carbon, hydrogen and oxygen. Presence of iron is required in the plant. Sulphur, potassium, phosphorus, calcium and other trace elements also play a role as glucose is converted into more complicated sugars, starches, fats, vitamins and structural cellulose that supports tiny shoots as well as giant trees. Some plants, especially the bean family, incorporate large quantities of nitrogen into their cells, thereby producing proteins along with the carbohydrates. Vitamin production and mineral content in plants add further nutritional value. I've been asked if growing methods affect a particular plant's nutritional values and flavor. As far as I can determine, only bulk may be affected. Other characteristics seem to depend primarily on inherited characteristics.

As a postscript it might be added that plants do not always photosynthesize their own food. Mushrooms, prized for their flavor, but not their food value, live in the dark on prefabricated food from other plants. Some parasitic plants drive their roots into the circulatory systems of green plants to obtain food. Yeasts and bacteria live on plant food originally produced in the light and, though they can be destructive, are instrumental in production of fine breads, cheeses and wines.

CIRCULATION

The vascular system of plants, especially the higher ones, is far different from the familiar heart, arteries and veins of warmblooded animals. How a plant like a tall tree can absorb water and salts from the ground and deliver them to leaves high in the air as well as distribute food manufactured in the leaves to all other parts down to the tiniest root hair is still not well understood, mainly because of the efficiency with which a plant overcomes gravity and the speed with which particular molecules travel from one part to another.

Generally speaking, sap travels upward through special cellular bundles called "xylem" (from Greek words meaning "woody structural components"), and nutrition is translocated through other vascular bundles known as "phloem" ("bark structural components"). The basic mechanism of circulation has been thought to be "diffusion," or the tendency for molecules, ions and atoms to be continually on the move, especially in liquids and gasses, so that they become completely intermingled. In a room of still air, perfume released in one corner is quickly noticed throughout the whole room. A droplet of liquid soap in a pan of water soon dissipates without stirring. But a plant is filled with barriers in the form of cell walls and is far different from a hollow tube of liquid. These walls are porous to a degree and are known as semi-permeable membranes, because they let only selected particles pass through. Water molecules and mineral salt ions dissolved therein can enter root surfaces, but most of the large organic molecules manufactured by the plant are too large to pass the other way. Diffusion becomes a one-way street known as "osmosis"; a force known as "osmotic pressure" develops, from cell to cell up to the leaves where pure water evaporates, not only cooling the plant, but also maintaining a high continual imbalance of larger molecules inside the plant. Osmosis may also occur on other plant surfaces with disastrous results, witness the literal explosion of tomato fruits after prolonged dry spells and then a heavy rain.

Traditionally, osmotic pressure has been thought of as the only driving force pushing sap upward, but it's not powerful enough. Distribution of food manufactured by the plant is generally downward and aided by gravity, but here too, diffusion through cell walls is unexpectedly fast. The rapidity of a plant's internal transport almost indicates that plants, like animals, have "heart pumps."

REPRODUCTION AND EVOLUTION

The simplest plants, such as yeasts, reproduce by cell division or by forming spores that travel by air or other means to grow in new locations. Since these new plants are identical to the original and no male or female organs are involved, such reproduction is known as asexual. Higher plants have many more choices. Leaves and stems—cuttings—can take root as can buds, either in the form of bulbs or as eyes of an underground stem (tuber) like the potato. Certain plants can be propagated by root cuttings or divisions, others by budding and grafting. All these methods are asexual, yielding duplicates of original plants. Seeds are the product of sexual reproduction and usually develop only if female ovaries are fertilized by male pollen. Surprisingly, this is not always true. Dandelions, for example, can sometimes produce seeds without pollination.

As edible plants evolved, animals, including man, first simply ate the leaves, flowers, stalks, fruits or seeds as they existed in the wild. Even today, of course, wild plants provide substantial quantities of food. Indians in Illinois and Wisconsin are said still to refuse to alter the natural life style of wild rice for religious reasons.

But long ago man learned that many wild plants could produce more abundantly if grown in cultivated soil, if he removed the rocks and broke up the clods of hard soil, if he watered, fertilized, weeded and otherwise cared for food-producing plants. He soon realized the advantages of saving the seeds of the healthiest, hardiest, most productive plants for sowing the next season's crop. Larger kernels of grain, as well as kernels especially suited to bread-making were developed as long ago as the early Egyptian era by such selectivity, though in the field of vegetables it was much later that production of seeds became a commercial enterprise. In the early 1800's the French firm of Vilmoring-Andrieux confidently offered "The World's First Selection" of vegetable seeds with "guaranteed" quality after extensively selecting only seeds from the finest plants for production in their experimental gardens.

Meanwhile farmers and gardeners in monasteries and on noblemen's vast estates were trying new soil mixtures, cultivating methods, composts and temperature controls. By the time of Columbus they were knowledgeable about cross-pollination of flowers and vegetables and intrigued with the results. New beauty, new flower shapes and colors, new succulence and increased hardiness sometimes resulted, but it seemed to be purely a matter of chance whether a crossbreed turned out to be a spectacular improvement or a dismal failure. Progress was slow for the next 400 years, even though the mechanics of pollination were fairly well understood. It was known that pollen developed in anthers in prodigious

quantities (now known to exceed 50 million on a single corn plant) and that the male pollen was transported to female stigmas of the same or different plants by gravity, breezes, water, insects or birds. In the tight flowers of most grains it was realized that this process occurred within each single plant. The pollen was known to grow in tubes down to the ovaries where fertilization was completed and seeds formed. The science of not only botany, but also horticulture was well under way, yet it was not understood why desirable inherited traits sometimes showed up in progeny and other times vanished.

In 1865, Gregor Mendel, a modest Austrian monk of the Augustinian order, who had earlier been sent to the University of Vienna to study mathematics and the natural sciences to become a teacher like other monks of his order, reported results of nine years' experimentation with ordinary garden peas. Botanists failed to grasp the significance of his conclusions. Horticulturists, already vigorously pursuing the economic rewards of seed and plant production, might have been more excited if one of their own had conducted such experiments, then exploited them. But Mendel died in 1884, his papers gathering dust, long before his name became so famous that in the since postulated theory of the role of chromosomes and genes in inheritance the latter are known as "Mendel's factor."

Mendel's breakthrough consisted of proving that inherited characteristics can be predicted with mathematical certainty and do not result from a toss of the dice. He concerned himself with such characteristics as whether pea seeds are round or wrinkled, yellow or green; whether flowers are red or white, axial or terminal; whether pods are green or yellow, inflated or constricted; whether stems are long or short. He found that first generation crossbreeds could resemble one parent alone, yet that in the next generation characteristics of the other grandparent would show up with mathematical predictability and that there were dominant and recessive characteristics.

It wasn't until 1900 that Mendel's papers were "rediscovered" almost simultaneously by De Vries in Holland, Correns in Germany and von Tschermak-Seysnegg in Austria. Horticulturalists and botanists both verified the validity of his conclusions and crop production since has gradually turned into a science. It took another 30 years for hybrid seeds to become widely available to farmers and gardeners, but their proliferation since has been astounding. Today growers of commercial crops as well as home gardeners can select flowers and vegetables tailor-made to fit particular conditions including growing season and to produce desired features in flower, fruit, leaf, stem or root.

A home gardener who contemplates saving seeds from a favorite plant should be warned that natural selection can be risky, since he is rarely dealing with pure strains, and the seeds he might save could produce plants quite different from the parent. Genetics is a science, a tricky one. Even experts who first try to develop new strains, then breed to fit a particular pattern, are many times unsuccessful. As an amateur, it's better to buy seeds or small plants from professionals and profit from their years of plant breeding. Then you can concentrate on the joy of watching them grow and produce delicacies under the loving care only you can offer.

PLANT PARTS

The nutritional value of vegetables varies as widely as their flavor, texture and bulk and depends greatly on when they are harvested and how soon after they are eaten. Some that offer little food value are delicious and crunchy, decorative in the garden and on the table. They can also provide the bulk so important in the human digestive process. Concentrated nutrition is only one of several criteria in deciding what to plant. Everyone knows that vegetables in various stages of growth provide carbohydrates, proteins and minerals in varying degrees as well as vitamins like A in green and yellow vegetables, E in green vegetables as well as in seed oils, K, B_2, B_6 and C (especially in tomatoes). A recent theory claims that a diet of natural carbohydrates in vegetables and fruits along with lower consumption of animal proteins and moderate exercise can actually reverse cardio-vascular diseases. While I'm not a vegetarian or a medical expert, I am a confirmed vegetable lover. I enjoy tilling the soil and respond to beauty of both vegetables and flowers. I'm also awed by the growing processes of plants in general and have a healthy appetite.

Vegetables store their own food in fascinating ways and for many purposes including survival, growth, environmental crises and reproduction. Pollen, ovaries, seeds, seed contain-

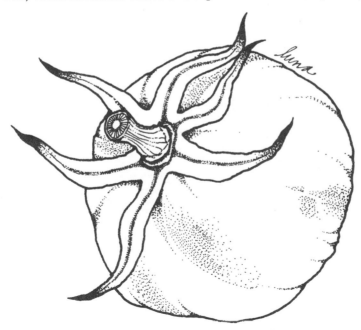

ers, sprouts, flowers, stems, leaves, buds, roots, rootlets, and root hairs are all not only growing parts of a sophisticated plant, but also components where food can be stored. Animals know this, of course, and often consume the food before the plant itself. Plants like bacteria often fight back.

Inconsequential parts of plants that are beneath the notice of herbivorous animals can be mind-boggling. One of the most spectacular partnerships occurs when bacteria living on the roots of bean plants convert nitrogen from the air into soluble molecules the plant converts into proteins. Roots are generally little understood, for they cannot be easily observed, though carrots are an exception. A cabbage plant may invade 200 cubic feet of soil. A corn stalk may spread roots over an area of four square feet, reaching down eight feet. A shallow squash may produce roots spreading over 20 square feet while growing down only a foot. A single stalk of winter rye is said to grow 5,000 miles of root hairs, or according to other sources 14 million root branches 380 miles long, plus 14 billion root hairs combining to provide 2500 square feet of surface area underground compared to 51 that meets the eye and the air.

Vegetables generally considered as root crops vary considerably. Carrots store giant amounts of food in their main root in anticipation of completing their biennial cycle, the second year being devoted to living primarily off the stored food and producing flowers and seeds. If faced with unusually bad growing conditions, they may use up their root food and go to seed in one season. Carrot tops have sometimes been used as substitutes for parsley, while some varieties of parsley produce sizeable roots with a distinctive flavor. Potatoes, as mentioned before, are swollen underground stems. Peanuts are really peas growing in pods on flower stalks that, after flowering, grow downward into the earth.

Edible parts above ground comprise seeds, seed containers, flowers, leaves and stalks. Peas and beans, of course, are seeds that may be eaten with or without their pods. The fruit of tomato and pepper plants contain hundreds of seeds, but it's the fleshy container that's loaded with delicious food. Artichokes are eaten as unripe flowers. Left to ripen they turn into pretty, purple, thistle-like blossoms. Cauliflower and broccoli are unripe flower clusters, the latter prized for its stems as well. Leaves of chard and spinach and their stems contrast with tighter leaves in the form of heads of cabbage and some lettuces. Celery and celery cabbage lie in between. Rhubarb, treated like a fruit in the kitchen, is different. Its leaves are bitter and considered to be poisonous. In the onion family shoots and bulbs (leaves modified for storage) are both utilized. Tender, edible shoots of asparagus bear little resemblance to the lacy mature stems with decorative berries, which are inedible.

The world of edible vegetables is varied indeed and undoubtedly will become even more so as plant breeders continue their experiments and introduce varieties which will outperform those presently available. New techniques such as radiation treatment and technological offshoots of diverse scientific programs are showing promise of plant improvement beyond what crossbreeding alone can accomplish.

As a home gardener, you will always have to consider not only what plants to grow in limited space, but also which varieties best suit your particular situation. However, never forget your garden is *yours*—to have fun with, to tailor to your own whims and fancies.

Vegetable Culture

The word "culture" can have two meanings that, at first glance, seem to be unrelated. It has come to mean enlightenment and excellence of taste as civilization advances, or, from earlier times I would guess, fostering the growth of living material in prepared nutriment media. It derives from the Latin "cultus" meaning "care," and its taking on a loftier meaning is similar to the way many words in our language probably started when man became intimately involved with plants, then were metaphorically broadened. "The ship plows the seas," "the flowering of New England" and "the fruit of man's labor" are but a few examples of "flowery" speech.

Vegetable growth, though dependent on basic characteristics of the environment and the seed or plant itself, is pretty much in the hands of the "caring" gardener. He can usually improve the environment, see that his plants have proper nutrients and moisture and protect them from predators. In a small garden he can train them to grow in special ways that conserve space.

SOIL

Though it contains largely mineral particles of silicon and aluminum compounds, soil to a plant is really a water-and-air growing medium found in the spaces between soil particles.

A good tilth—that is, the preparation of a crumbly mixture of these soil particles, not too small and not too large, together with substantial quantities of organic material—is not easy in many yards or, for that matter, on many farms. Good soil of suitable depth is a rare natural commodity on the earth's surface.

It took aeons for winds, rains, glaciers, chemical action, wild plants and animals to build up a very thin layer of fine topsoil on fairly level earth surfaces. Long before man's exploitation of fertile areas natural forces often washed such soil into the seas or drove it far down into crevices. The same forces that eroded mountains and ground rocks into gravel, sand, silt or clay were not only adding to the soil, but also taking away. Then came early man, who, for example, in the Middle East little understood the necessity of preserving the quality of the soil, who turned lush valleys into deserts by overcultivation without fertilizing. In the 1930's the great plain states of America became vulnerable to drought and winds because hardy, natural grasses had been replaced by seasonal grains on thousands of square miles of plowed, fertile land. Topsoil in the United States is thought to have averaged nine inches in the 1700's, today about six. Now, contour plowing, terracing and damming of rivers help save precious soil during minor floods, but can be ineffective if Nature goes on a major rampage. Droughts like that in central Africa in 1974-75 are also well beyond man's control.

However, in small world gardening you can tackle soil problems much as your ancestors did, add a few tricks of more recent vintage and develop good soil. If, as you first view your potential vegetable garden area, you see a fine stand of grass or varied weeds (the presence of only one variety may indicate soil deficiencies to which it has adapted) you may consider yourself lucky. The chances are that drainage is good, light is adequate, enough moisture is retained and nutriments have not been leached out. Either previous gardeners, Nature, or both have been kind. Spading may reveal numerous earthworms that not only dig holes in the soil as they feed on decayed organic matter, but produce castings of "digested" crumbly soil and waste products up to 10 tons an acre per year beneficial to plants. The soil in such an area may even approach an ideal loam, a balanced mixture of clay, silt, sand and decayed or undecayed organic material (with bacteria actively turning the latter into the former, true humus that holds soil together in crumbs). Such loam is porous enough to absorb moisture rapidly, yet retain it well; roots easily penetrate and grow; chemically it is neither too acid nor too alkaline. It is easily spaded, surface cultivated or weeded. It's not too muddy in the spring or baked hard in the summer. Small amounts of fertilizers are easily introduced and distributed to roots, rootlets and root hairs; heavy fertilizing is not necessary. If you start with such soil, growing fine vegetables will be simple, providing you revitalize the area annually by crop rotation and replace most of the nutriments that the plants take from the earth. Just because you start with good soil doesn't mean you can willy nilly grow crops in it year after year, but with a little care it will never turn into a desert.

Chances are in your situation, however, the garden area is far from ideal—it may lie on a slope, it may be that it's rocky, that it's loaded with heavy clay, that it's mostly loose sand or, if it surrounds a newly built house, the good looking, artificially positioned topsoil is only a few inches deep. If it is not almost level, first consideration should be given to terracing, which in a small area almost always calls for retaining walls. Initial spading should be at least 12 inches deep to find out what vegetable roots will be faced with. Coarse gravel, small stones and large rocks should, of course, be removed and either hauled away or saved for path or retaining wall construction. Builders often bury cast-aside construction materials or use them for fill. Get rid of them. If you run into occasional clods of very heavy clay, they should be treated like rocks, though it may be worthwhile to consider breaking them up later and gradually incorporating them into compost heaps. (If the clay is capable of being broken up, it's worth working with.) By this time you've become well enough acquainted with your soil to guess whether its mixture of mineral particles and organic material fits into a desirable range you can work with or will heed corrective action.

TYPES OF SOIL
In order to understand the process by which soils are made more productive, it is essential to consider the basic types of soil, their characteristics and which crops are best suited to each type.

Clay
Because clay soil is constituted of many small particles which bind together when dry, forming an extremely hard mass, it does not encourage either air or water penetration. Consequently, clay soil warms very slowly during the spring months but retains the warmth well into the fall. It is generally rich in plant nutrients. Crops which do well in clay are celery, cabbages, leeks, peas, beans and rhubarb. Lettuce may be grown in clay as well, provided the surface of the soil will absorb the moisture this green requires. This is especially true of those varieties of lettuce which have a large leaf surface and shallow roots, as they tend to lose moisture through evaporation.

The addition of organic material such as peat moss, well-rotted compost, dung, steer manure, sawdust, sand, or wood chips to clay soil will help increase water and air absorption. Green manuring is another method of improving clay soil. Sow clover, vetch or other leguminous crops late in the summer. Allow the vegetation to reach a height of four to five inches. Then incorporate it into the soil by digging. The digging itself is a great help in opening the soil. Leave the surface in a rough condition. The winter rain and frost will break up large clods and by spring the soil should be in a greatly improved condition.

Never dig clay soil to the same depth in two consecutive cultivations. The constant use of a rotovater set to the same level will form a "hard pan." As the layer below cultivation becomes harder and harder, water will cease penetrating and concentrations of salts and fertilizer drained from above will form. As a result plant roots will suffer tremendously. Periodic deep digging and/or the cultivation of deep-rooted plants, such as potatoes, will prevent this situation from developing.

Silt

Silt soil has the same negative characteristics as clay without the prime advantage of rich food reserves. Therefore, it must be supplemented by additions of fertilizer, which should be applied in the spring of the year.

Because the soil itself is made up of larger particles than that of clay, it may be cultivated earlier in the spring and later into the fall. Silt soils will vary in color from tan to red to grey.

Sandy

Particles of sand soil vary in size from .05 to 1.0 millimeters, the latter being a fine gravel. Sandy soil allows good drainage and air circulates through it freely. It warms rapidly in the spring but tends to lose heat early in the fall. Sandy soil is easily cultivated but, due to the excellent drainage inherent in its composition, plant food is lost and the soil tends toward dryness. An addition of large quantities of organic matter will help to reduce loss of moisture. Organic matter should be worked down to a good depth, as plant roots will go deeper in sandy soil. Both salad and root crops do very well in this type of soil.

Loam

Loam is the name given to soil which is made up of sand, silt and clay particles. Even proportions of each would constitute the ideal soil but this rarely occurs. Loam does, however, embody the positive qualities of each type of soil. All loams contain a good supply of organic matter. Loamy soils are found where the land has been under cultivation for many years and where the correct attention has been paid to its maintenance.

Peat

Peat is a soil composed of decayed matter, usually mosses, grasses or ferns. Lake beds and bogs, forested areas, sites where cattle were quartered and land where flooding deposited

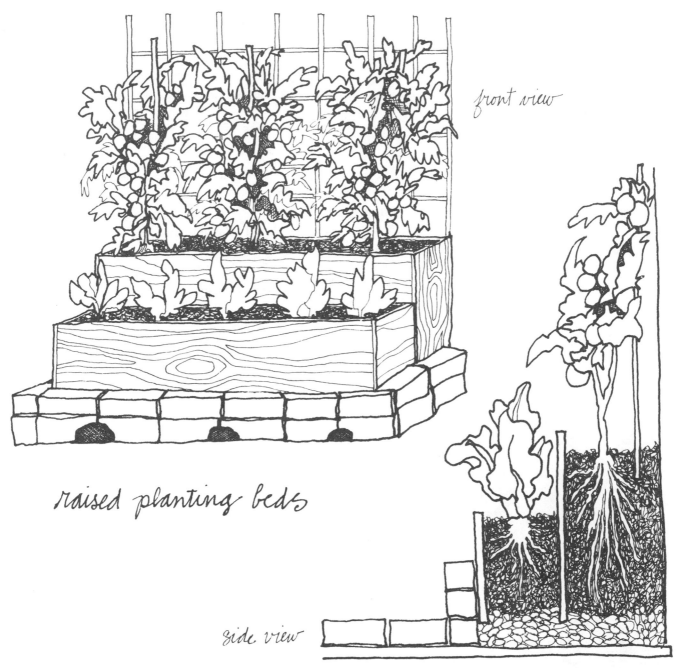

front view

raised planting beds

side view

quantities of vegetation are all composed of peat soil. While obviously rich in plant nutrients, this type of soil may be lacking in a correct mineral balance which plants require for healthy growth.

In general it is not essential for the home gardener to have an analysis done to determine the mineral content of the soil. If the ground is well cultivated and a wide variety of crops are grown the soil should balance itself.

pH

Neutral soil has a pH of seven. This is the same pH as clean pure water. A soil which is above the level of seven is alkaline, below the level of seven is acid. Most plants thrive in a pH between five and a half and six and a half.

Alkaline soils are found in dry regions where the calcium and magnesium are not leached out through heavy rains. The alkalinity of soil can be further increased if the water used is high in salts. Hence, commercially softened water shouldn't be used in the garden.

Acid soils occur where there is a high concentration of humus which has not been aerated, in a region of stagnate water or where there has been little cultivation.

Alkaline soils can be brought into a better balance by the addition of peat moss, leaf mold, grass clippings or bark dust. In severe cases, a light application of sulphur, which is incorporated into the soil by digging, may be necessary. Caution is advised when employing this particular method and the pH level must be tested after each application. You can purchase a pH testing kit at any nursery or garden center.

Heavy flooding of the ground can also lower the alkalinity of the soil. This method is useless unless there is very good drainage all the way down to the subsoil. If the soil is porous to a depth of two or three feet, this leaching process will work well.

The addition of dolomite limestone, which contains calcium and magnesium, is used in correcting high levels of acidity in the soil. Liming should never be considered a substitute for fertilizing. The lime will provide the alkalinity which allows soil bacteria to break down available food for plants, but in itself it is not plant food. After an application of lime, however, less fertilizer is needed because of the release of the reservoirs of plant food by the more active bacteria. Lime should be applied every two years, two weeks prior to the planting of crops. Never mix it with fertilizer. Certain crops, when planted in a soil which tends toward high acidity, need a good dressing of lime worked into the ground before they will produce abundantly. These crops include peas, beans, turnips and cabbage. The chemicals in lime help break down clay soil particles, but give body to sandy soil.

CULTIVATION OF THE SOIL

Single Spit Digging This simple operation changes the position of the top nine inches of soil, actually turning it upside down. To start, define the area which is to be dug. Spread a layer of compost or other organic material, no more than four inches thick, over the ground. Open a trench 10 to 12 inches wide and nine inches deep across one end. Remove all soil and place it at the end of the area to be dug. Place a layer of compost in the bottom of the trench. Spade the next four or five inches of soil along the length of the trench and, as you dig out, turn it upside down. Continue along until the first trench is filled with the earth dug from the second. The last trench should be filled with the soil from the first.

This operation is best done in the fall so that the winter weather can act upon the turned ground. Try to keep the ground fairly level as you dig in order to avoid a lot of leveling at the time of planting.

Trenching Begin as with single spit digging, but make the trench six to 10 inches wider. Fork over the bottom of the trench, incorporating compost or other organic matter into the soil. Even if no organic matter is used, the benefits of trenching will still be noticeable. As a result of this operation, the soil will be cultivated to a depth of 18 to 24 inches. The overall volume of the soil is increased, thus allowing the roots deeper penetration, strengthening plants and promoting overall health and productiveness.

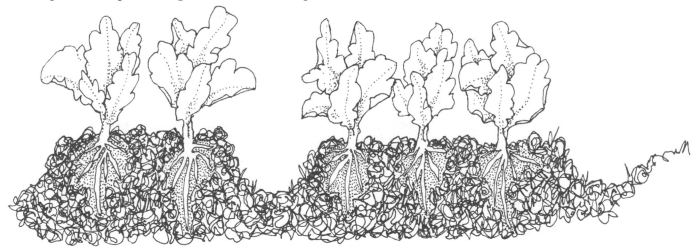

trenches and beds

A few basic rules must be followed in both digging and trenching. Insert the spade at a 90-degree angle. Do not lift the spade of soil until it has been cut on both sides and at the back. Do not overtax muscles unused to such work by digging over long periods of time. If the digging is done in the fall the ground should be left in a "rough" condition. This allows the action of winter weather, rain, snow and frost, to penetrate the soil and break up hard clods. In spring, when sowing is done, the soil will be easier to level and will produce a finer tilth, or texture, than if you level at the time of the digging process. The addition of compost to very hard soils, such as clay, should be made in vertical layers instead of horizontal ones. This is done by placing the compost against the sides of the trench away from you and the next spadeful of earth up against the layer of compost. In this manner, air and water can penetrate more easily.

Digging should be done after each harvest. In well-prepared soil, spading is unnecessary and simple turning with a fork will suffice. Always remove any stones or roots.

Preparation of Soil after Digging or Trenching Level the ground with a spade or fork, making sure there are no obvious hills and valleys. Rake the soil with the teeth at a 90-degree angle, removing any debris such as stones or large lumps of soil. These preparations will bring the soil to a cultivated state for planting.

If you are going to plant from seed another few steps will be necessary. Firm the ground by walking on it, rake again and repeat, until the top three inches of earth are free of large lumps, level and uniform enough to run a stick through. If the surface is dry, sprinkle it, being cautious not to overwater.

SEED SOWING OUT OF DOORS

Make a drill by using the corner of a hoe blade which is inserted into the soil to the desired depth. Pull toward you until the drill is made. If only a very shallow drill is required, use a stick instead of a hoe. If a deep or wide drill is necessary, use the full blade of the hoe. Sow the seed into the bottom of the drill. Start with wide spacing, going back over the area several times, until the seed is well distributed along the row.

After sowing, replace into the drill the soil piled on the sides. Firm the soil lightly with the end of a rake. Water the rows making sure the soil is not displaced by too heavy a flow from the hose. Label the rows with the variety of vegetable and the date planted. In this way you can determine how long the seed takes to germinate, aiding greatly with future planning. Birds are often a problem in the case of shallow sowings. Place small sticks at

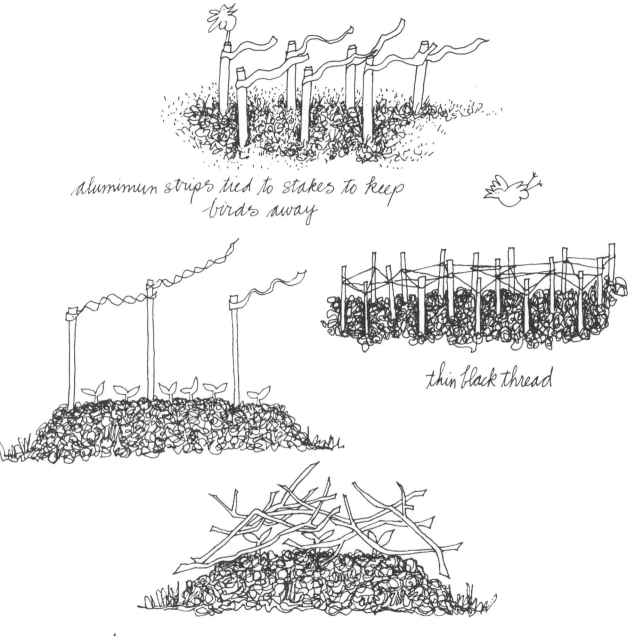

aluminum strips tied to stakes to keep
birds away

thin black thread

twigs or branches to protect seedlings from birds

irregular intervals into the soil over the sown seed. String black thread between the sticks. The birds will brush their wings against the thread, be disturbed and forget about the seed.

Thinning

Crops are either started in seedbeds or sown directly in the beds from which they will be harvested. Root crops planted in place must be thinned out as soon as the seedlings reach a height of a few inches. This thinning allows space for the remaining seedlings to develop to a healthy maturity. The tender, sweet thinnings of many root crops, such as beets and carrots, are delectable in salads.

Growing Seedlings in Beds for Transplanting

Certain crops, such as cabbage, leeks, onions and peppers, can be sown in separate seedbeds, best located in a sunny but sheltered spot, and when the seedlings are four to six inches high, lifted and transplanted to rows in the garden.

Water the seedbed the day before transplanting the seedlings. Place a fork a few inches away from the side of the row and gently lift the plant, being careful to avoid damaging the roots. Handle the plants with care. Mark the position where they are to be planted and, using a trowel, dig a hole to accommodate all the roots of the plant without crowding. Replace the soil around the plant and water each plant thoroughly. This assures close root-soil contact. It is best to plant on a cloudy day or in the evening. This will allow the plant time to settle in before being exposed to the full brunt of a hot sun. If very hot weather prevails, cover the newly transplanted seedlings with awnings of paper or light cloth to give some protection. This can be done by attaching these materials to small lightweight stakes placed near the seedlings.

SEED SOWING INDOORS

Seeds are like wound-up clocks. They start to work releasing all the elements necessary for growth when conditions are right. Three things are necessary: water, air and adequate temperature. Water softens the seed coat so that stored food may be released and the cells fattened. Air, well circulated, allows the seed to breathe and activates cell growth. The correct temperature makes for optimum activity inside the seed.

As most seeds are small, the soil mixture into which they are sown should be fine, containing no stones or large lumps of earth. If there is any doubt about the cleanliness of the soil being used, you can sterilize small amounts at home. First allow the soil to dry.

Place one-half-inch water in the bottom of a large saucepan. Bring the water to a boil and add the soil. Simmer for 15 minutes and cool. Or the soil can be placed dry in a heavy-duty plastic oven bag and baked for one hour at 180°. A soil mix made up of the following proportions is good for seed sowing. It should be passed through one-fourth-inch mesh screening and mixed well before sowing the seed. You may use either a household sieve or a wooden frame covered with screening.

> Two parts loam (A good potting mix sold in nurseries or topsoil
> from the garden will be quite adequate.)
> One part peat moss (This will hold moisture.)
> One part coarse builders' sand (This creates an open
> mixture which allows air and heat to enter and facilitates
> the draining of surplus water.)

Seed Sowing in Containers

It is essential that any container used for growing plants be clean. Clay pots, wooden or plastic flats or milk cartons are all acceptable. Use your imagination when selecting the container you are going to use, but be sure the container is clean and without traces of former plant-residents' problems such as fungi and bacteria. This will require a good scrubbing with soapy water and a mild solution of bleach. Also make sure there is ample drainage at the bottom of the container. Gravel, stones or pieces of broken pots are all fine for this purpose. Cover this material with the soil mixture, stopping within one inch of the top. Firm gently, making sure of even firmness over the complete surface. Sow seed thinly.

vegetable crate

dairy containers

33

If the seed you are starting is very fine, mix it with a fine sand before sowing. This allows you to easily see the seed sown. Do not neglect the corners of the containers. Cover the seed evenly with the same soil mixture. The depth of cover will vary with size of the seed. A basic rule of thumb is to cover about three times the height of the seed when it is lying flat.

After sowing and covering, water in, using a sprinkler can or placing the container in water so water level is just below the rim. Once the surface becomes moistened, the container should be removed from the water. Cover the container with a piece of glass or clear plastic to help conserve moisture and heat. Place newspaper over the glass or plastic to protect the surface from direct sun. Check the soil surface daily, making sure it has not become dry and water if necessary. As soon as signs of germination are evident remove the paper and, in a few days, the glass.

Location of the container is important. If placed on a window ledge or other sunny spot, check the edges directly hit by the sun to make sure no excessive drying is taking place. Ideal temperature would be around 65°F. Thin the seedlings when they begin to germinate, removing the weakest ones so the remaining have room to develop. When the seedlings are a size that can be handled with ease (two to three inches high), it is time to "prick" them out into another container.

Pricking Out Seedlings

Now that the seeds have started to grow, more nourishment must be provided. There are many soil mixes recommended. One of the best is *seven parts loam, three parts peat moss (leaf mold may be used) and two parts of builders' sand.* To this mixture add Osmocote or a small amount of other commercial fertilizer; a formula of 10-7-4 would be suitable. Mix all the ingredients together thoroughly and fill a new larger, deeper container with the soil mix, firming it slightly.

Make holes with a dibble, sharpened stick or pencil in the soil. The holes should be spaced so the seedlings have enough room to develop into the desired planting size. This distance will vary from crop to crop but will normally be about three inches. Remove the seedlings from the original container, being very cautious not to disturb the delicate roots. This can be done by placing a dibble or similar construction at a 45-degree angle to the seedling, gently pushing it toward the roots and popping the seedling out of the soil in a smooth motion. Place the seedling into the prepared hole and firm down gently.

Certain crops, such as squash, cucumbers and tomatoes, are best sown directly into small pots. These plants do not like to be disturbed and do better if they are allowed to grow on steadily. Use the same 7-3-2 soil mixture described above, but instead of transplanting, sow three seeds to a pot and remove the weakest seedlings, leaving one per pot to grow.

Sowing seed indoors under warmer conditions allows earlier sowing and thus earlier planting. If growing in an area where light is available from one direction only, be sure to turn the plants in order that they may grow straight. Plants always lean toward the light.

During all the procedures described, never let the plants become dry. Try to keep the temperature even, avoiding extreme changes at all costs. As the plants grow, gradually move them to cooler areas so that after four or five weeks they are growing in conditions similar to what they will experience when planted out.

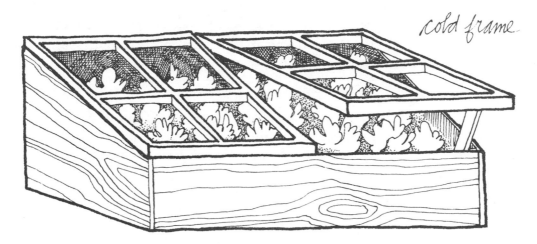

cold frame

Cold Frames and Hot Beds

If you have room in your garden, a cold frame is the ideal structure to aid in the adjustment of seedlings from indoor to outdoor temperatures. The cold frame is most often made of wood and can be described simply as a bottomless box with a removable top of glass or heavy clear plastic. The frame is sunk into the ground so the structure slopes, the front being about two inches shorter than the back. The cold frame's heat source is the sun, and as the days warm up the top is opened for longer periods each day so the plants do not overheat. Before the seedlings are planted out, you should be able to leave the top off all day and night. Putting seedlings in a cold frame for even a few days after germinating them in higher temperatures should make them able to withstand the vagaries of outdoor weather much more easily.

In very coldest weather you may decide a hot bed is needed. The structure is like that of the cold frame, but an electric heating coil is installed in the bottom of the bed, covered with soil to a depth of about six inches and then monitored by a thermostat.

Planting out Indoor-Grown Plants
Having weaned the young plants to outdoor conditions, plant on a day when the sun is neither too hot nor too bright. Actually, a cloudy day is ideal for this procedure. Make sure the soil is well worked and wet it down before planting. Prepare holes slightly larger than the seedlings' root masses and with a trowel, remove the plants from the flat to the ground or final container. Try not to disturb the roots during this operation. Firm the plants in the ground and water in well. If the temperatures are at all extreme, protect the plants for the first few days with paper or light cloth. Make sure that the plants do not dry out. Beware of strong winds as they can cause excessive drying.

CLOCHES
While it is not possible to erect a permanent structure over an entire garden, there are structures that can be used to protect plants from inclement weather. The cloche is one of the most convenient of these. Bell-shaped glass cloches have been used for centuries, especially by the French. Tent- and barn-shaped cloches, much like miniature greenhouses, are an invention of the English and were developed at the turn of the century. These cloches are constructed of glass, plastic or polyethylene on a wire frame.

Planting may be done a few weeks earlier than normal if cloches are used. The crops will grow more quickly and the time to maturity will be shortened considerably with this added protection. Cloches are relatively easy to move (especially the lightweight plastic ones), so they may be placed end to end to shelter a complete row and then moved to another row when necessary. Two, three or more rows of cloches may be erected in the garden, depending upon need. When not in use, the cloches fold up and store flat.

If ready-made cloches are not available in your area, check the source list at the back of this book or create a comparable structure yourself with heavy-gauge wire and glass or plastic panels.

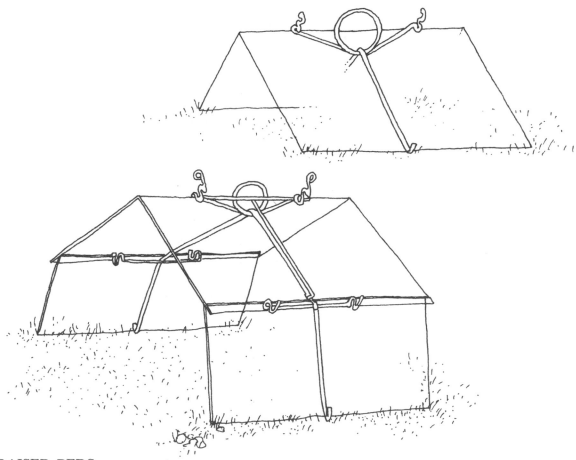

RAISED BEDS

Sometimes, due to removal of soil during construction, complete absence of soil or extreme alkalinity or acidity, it is necessary to use the raised bed method of growing. A raised bed is also an excellent way to convert a paved surface, such as driveway or patio, into a vegetable garden. First delineate the area to be used. The actual size of the raised beds is determined by the size and shape of the lot. Four feet wide by eight feet long is a good size. A border of wood or brick can be placed around the section. It should be high enough and sturdy enough to contain the soil. A minimum depth of 12 inches of soil is required for most plants. If at all possible work over the surface of the existing ground before adding the new soil. Even breaking the surface to a depth of a few inches helps in improving the drainage.

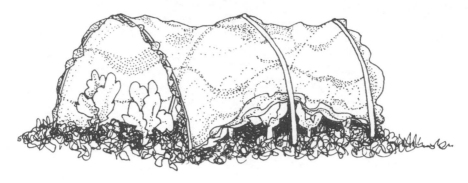

temporary plastic greenhouse secured with bamboo or wire

When planning raised beds, allow enough room for a path to accommodate the gardener and a wheelbarrow, if necessary. Water outlets should be available as well.

The best topsoil should be used to fill the beds. Make sure that you see a sample of the soil at the time of purchase so it can be compared with what is ultimately delivered. If you desire, peat moss and sand can be added to the topsoil you purchase. A good proportional mixture would be seven parts topsoil, three parts peat moss and two parts sand. Mix very thoroughly before putting into the beds.

Raised beds tend to warm earlier in spring and cool more rapidly in fall. In some raised beds you might consider placing warming cables in the ground to hasten the spring warming and extend the fall season. This way you will be able to sow seed a little earlier in the spring and to harvest your vegetables a little later into the fall. It is important to check raised beds regularly to make sure the soil is moist. The lack of depth in these beds causes the soil to dry out rapidly because often there is no subsoil moisture which can be drawn from below and utilized.

MULCHING

Mulching both conserves soil moisture and keeps weeds to a minimum. Each plant in a given area takes moisture from the soil. If weeds occupy space with the desired crop they utilize a share of the moisture available in that space, leaving less for the crop. Weeds also require food for growth and deplete the store of nutrients in the soil.

There are a variety of materials which can serve as mulches. Some even add a decorative aspect to the garden. Any of the following are good: bark chips, sawdust, peat

moss, shredded newspapers, cocoa hulls, straw, lawn clippings (these should be spread in thin layers so as not to cake together and decompose) and compost (providing no weed seeds are mixed in). Though plastic is favored by some for mulching, it can cause problems and I do not recommend its use. While it does keep the soil moist and keeps down weed germination, air cannot enter the soil as it should. This can cause the soil to sour, become too compact and be in poor condition when the plastic is removed.

Mulches should be applied in the spring, once the soil has begun to warm up. If done too early, the mulch will simply trap the cold in the soil. It is also important that the soil be moist before the mulch is applied, otherwise there will be no moisture to keep in. Mulches should be evenly distributed over the surface; a two-inch depth is sufficient for fine mulch materials and no more than a four-inch depth for coarser ones. In this manner rain and air can penetrate. Winter mulches are used in extreme climates to protect established plants against severe freezing.

Fine mulches should be incorporated into the soil at the time of the annual digging. Large materials, such as bark chips, should be raked aside and replaced after cultivation. As the mulches break down they do tend to sap the nitrogen from the soil, competing with the plant material for this nutrient. Adding a little extra nitrogen to the soil when applying fertilizers will compensate for any such loss.

FRENCH INTENSIVE METHOD

Many current garden books mention the French intensive method as a practical and successful way to increase crop yield in a garden of limited space. The procedure is described as one in which a high proportion of organic material is incorporated into the soil, permitting plants to be grown closer together because of the greater concentration of needed nutrients. Faster growth also results, and more frequent harvests are realized from the available ground. The true French intensive method, however, is somewhat more complex than this. It was developed at the turn of the century in response to the demands of the marketplace.

Before the advent of greenhouse heating systems, a method was needed which would ready crops for market earlier in the season. Competition between growers generated the idea of exploiting an abundant natural product—horse manure. Around the Paris area there was always an ample supply of this product, since the horse was the most common means of transporting people and goods. Farmers soon realized that the heat produced by the fermentation of the dung would aid crop production: It would overcome the problem of cold temperatures and shorten maturation time. In many cases crops could be forced to maturity many weeks before they would otherwise be available.

Large quantities of fresh horse dung mixed with straw were placed in rows. This dung was turned over until the offensive smell had lessened and the high point of heat had passed. The dung was then spread out in layers varying in thickness anywhere from four feet to one foot. A layer of soil about six inches thick was placed on top of the dung, and sloped, glass-topped wooden frames were placed on the soil. The gardeners could then either place seed flats in the frames, which could then be transferred to the soil of another frame when the plants were ready, or plant young plants directly in the soil, their root tips reaching to the organic matter. The plants grown in these frames were protected from frost by the heat generated from the dung and contained by the frames, and at the same time growth was speeded up by the abundance of organic nutrients in the growing medium.

The length of time which a layer of dung provided heat was determined by its depth. For instance, a four-foot thick layer built up in January would provide heat for three to four months. By April its effectiveness had lessened considerably but it still protected plants from frost.

This method was so efficient that a nighttime temperature of 65°F could be maintained, allowing crops to be harvested much earlier than the norm. When all danger of frost had passed, the plants could be planted and glass frames removed. The plants which had enjoyed this extra warmth and abundant food supply grew at a fast rate—a very *intensive* production.

Today it is difficult to duplicate such heavy use of manure, but it is possible to augment the soil with very heavy doses of organic material to produce much the same result. Soil that is enriched far beyond the norm allows the gardener better use of limited space: the distance between plantings can be greatly reduced, and the maturation process is speeded up considerably, which permits more crops to be planted during a season. It must be noted, however, that problems can also occur. Intensive cropping can create overcrowding, which cuts down on much needed air circulation and increases the likelihood of diseases in the garden. Also, the idea of "catch-cropping" such quick-maturing vegetables as radishes and lettuce between rows is not possible. The intensive method, though, should be tried in the small world garden, especially with leaf and root crops which adapt well to it.

GARDENING UNDER LIGHTS

It is possible to raise good crops of vegetables under lights. However, considering the dollars spent in fuel and equipment, I do not think it is an economically worthwhile project. But if you want to have certain salad vegetables out of season, want a fascinating pastime or would like to delight your friends with a special treat at dinner, then growing vegetables under lights will provide hours of enjoyment.

There are many specially designed electric lamps on the market which provide the full spectrum of light needed by plants. Fluorescent tubes produce the blue and red rays and the regular incandescent bulb produces red and far-red rays. The best ratio of fluorescent to incandescent for a balanced light supply is on the order of two watts of fluorescent lighting to one of incandescent. For example, 100 watts of fluorescent lighting and 40 watts of incandescent would give the balanced ratio of light needed to grow plants to maturity. If you plan on starting vegetables from seed to bring them on to a size where they can be grown outdoors, then incandescent bulbs alone can work. In general, a light unit that provides 20 watts of light for each square foot of growing area will be adequate for raising vegetables.

Many consider the cool-white fluorescent tube the best for plants. Others suggest mixing the cool-white with daylight fluorescents for additional blue rays, which encourage foliage. You will have to experiment to find what works best for your plants. It is, however, recommended that you use the shorter fluorescent tubes as the light intensity diminishes markedly at the ends of the tubes.

How many hours of light need you provide your plants? Light requirements vary for each plant, but for the great majority of plants 14 to 16 hours of light are sufficient for healthy growth. An automatic timer will help maintain the plants' schedules.

One thing to watch is the temperature. The distance between the light source and the plants has to be carefully judged and constantly adjusted. With the specially designed growth lamps or fluorescents, four to six inches distance is generally fine. If you are using incandescents, they should be set at a greater distance, about 12 inches, or the heat buildup may burn the plants.

Because the prescribed distance between lights and plants must be maintained, as the plants grow the lights will have to be raised or the plants and their containers will need to be lowered to accommodate the new growth. This can be done by having the lights suspended from a chain or line which can be shortened as the need arises, or by having the container unit constructed on removable blocks for adjusting the height.

Plants growing under lights require closer attention to watering than those in the greenhouse or in containers outside. There will be a greater loss of moisture and the plants should be checked each day.

As the two main ingredients for fungi are present, moisture and heat, make sure there is adequate air flow to keep the surface of the plants dry. A small fan can provide this and will also prevent too much heat from building up around the plants.

For the gardener with a limited growing area outdoors or a short growing season, starting seedlings under lights can be of great assistance in maximizing outdoor land use. Sow the seed approximately six weeks before they are to be set outside. The soil mix to be used for the seedlings should be three parts loam or topsoil, two parts peat moss and one part builders' sand. Mix well and do not use any fertilizer in the seed sowing mix. As soon as the seedlings have germinated and are large enough to handle, prick them out into a soil mix of seven parts loam or topsoil, three parts peat moss and two parts builders' sand. If the plants are going to stay more than two to three weeks in these containers, add a slow release fertilizer to the soil mix. Because this fertilizer lasts for several months, when you plant outside it will continue to nourish the plants until they are established and can draw on the supply of food in the soil. As the temperatures inside will be much warmer than in the garden, be sure to harden the plants off by gradually lowering their environmental temperature before moving them to their permanent outdoor positions.

Should you wish to grow plants to maturity under lights, proceed as above but transplant the young plants into large containers that are at least 12 inches deep. Fill the container with the 7-3-2 mix after you have placed a layer of drainage material, such as gravel or small rocks, in the bottom. In view of the need for more frequent watering with this type of gardening, provide adequate drainage holes in the bottom of the container.

Because of the proximity of plants and the pleasant temperature, pest and disease control programs must be established and applied at the first sign of trouble. Pests can multiply quickly under these conditions and spread to all the plants.

Apart from the raising of seedlings for planting outdoors, the best vegetables to grow under lights are the salad crops—lettuce, radish—and the full range of herbs. This would include chives, sweet basil, parsley, sweet marjoram and sage. It is pleasant to be able to pick fresh herbs during the winter months, and then as soon as spring seed sowing time comes along to take these herbs from their "under lights" location and grow them outdoors.

A plant which does well under lights and has a somewhat unusual culture is watercress, *Nasturtium officinale.* This plant grows wild in streams and while not easily grown outdoors in the garden, does do well under lights. Grow watercress in a mixture of one part sand to eight parts peat moss. Place some horticultural charcoal in the bottom of a container, fill with the soil mix and thinly sow the watercress seeds. Because of the quick-growing nature of this plant, do not use a slow release fertilizer in the soil; instead, each time you water add some liquid fertilizer. The plants will start producing small leaves about three weeks after sowing. The best growing temperature is around 65°F and the central shoots should be pinched back to encourage bushiness. The most important thing to remember when growing watercress is to keep the growing medium constantly moist.

Remember that growing plants under lights is not the most economical way to raise vegetables to maturity. I do not recommend it except for starting seed for planting outdoors, especially in the short-growing season areas, and for keeping herbs growing during the winter, or, of course, as a pleasant hobby.

FERTILIZERS

It is not the purpose of this book to examine the subject of fertilizers in great detail. It is necessary, however, to understand the basics of fertilizers: what it is that they supply to the plant, the needs of certain plants for a particular fertilizer and what types of fertilizers to apply and when. This information will help you select the fertilizer best suited to each crop.

Plants need three main foods: nitrogen, phosphorus and potash. Natural fertilizers such as cow dung, horse dung and chicken manure contain all of these essential ingredients. If any of these are to be used they should be well rotted and thus free of any offensive odor. Any of these natural products used before they are well rotted will also cause plants to burn, as the concentration of certain of their ingredients is still too "hot." This is especially true of poultry manure. A look at the primary food demands of plants and how they utilize the nutrients supplied them will help in understanding the fertilizer requirements of your garden.

Nitrogen This food, which is listed on fertilizer packages as "N," makes plants grow quickly and keeps them green. It can be supplied in different forms: organically with blood meal, hoof and horn meal, fish emulsion, bone meal and inorganically with sulphate of ammonia and nitrate of soda. The percentage of nitrogen in these is usually indicated on the box. Sometimes the amount of water-soluble nitrogen which can be absorbed by the roots and, in turn, used by the plant, is less than the total percent listed on the box. Read the label carefully. Some of these fertilizers will also have percentages of other foods listed. For example, bone meal also contains phosphorus. This food, however, is released over a long period of time.

Do not apply nitrogenous food until just before planting, as the rains can cause leaching from the soil. Because nitrogen makes plants grow quickly, it is needed in higher proportion by leaf crops such as lettuce and cabbages.

Phosphorus Listed as "P" in fertilizer formulas, phosphorus is used by the plant in its flowering process, for strengthening the roots and during the process of internal food transference. If you are using an organic fertilizer such as dung, you will have to augment it with phosphates, as the animals retain most of that element in their own bodies. As it is used to strengthen roots, it is an important food to incorporate into the soil if you are growing any root crops such as turnips or beets, etc. Fertilizers containing phosphates tend to cause an acid reaction in the soil. If the soil is already on the low pH or acid side, lime should be used in conjunction with but not as a substitute for the fertilizer to counteract. If the soil is alkaline this acid reaction is beneficial in bringing down the pH to more tolerable levels. Phosphates remain in the soil a long time, not being leached as readily as nitrogen and therefore it is not essential to apply them each time the ground is cultivated.

Potash Listed as "K" in fertilizer formulas, potash plays an important part in each function of plant growth. It is utilized during the process of photosynthesis, where starch and sugars are manufactured from carbon dioxide and water. While potash is present in all soils, concentrations are higher in clay. If the balance between N, P and K is correct, plants will grow satisfactorily. If potash is abnormally high, stunting of plant growth will occur. Potash is usually applied as muriate of potash or sulphate of potash. Potash is also found in wood ashes. The ashes from your hearth are a valuable addition to the compost heap.

Slow release fertilizers These fertilizers are formulated to degrade slowly, allowing a continuous release of plant foods. One application of such a fertilizer may last as long as nine months. Though the added processes needed to prepare these fertilizers result in a higher cost, their use precludes frequent applications of plant food. This factor is a great advantage in container gardening. Osmocote is a slow release product which is highly recommended.

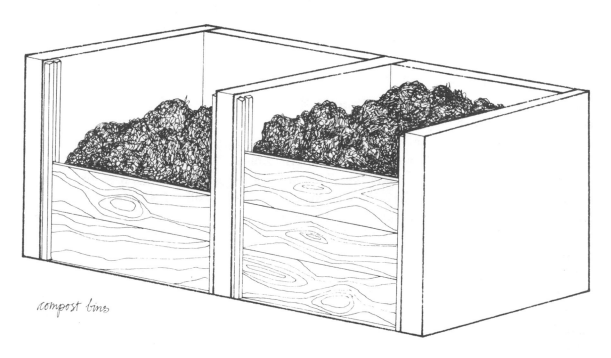

compost bins

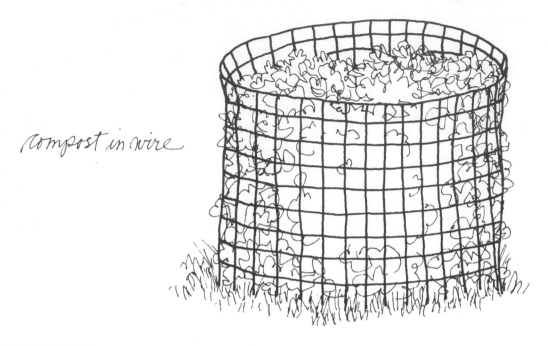

compost in wire

COMPOST HEAPS

Humus is a scarce commodity but, as previously explained, is necessary in all soils. Dung is a type of humus which is not readily available, and peat moss, obtained from bogs in Canada and the United States, is becoming rarer as bogs become exhausted. Compost of organic matter should be collected to augment the supply of humus in the soil.

Composting can be done in bins constructed of wood, stone, wire or brick, or combinations of these materials. There must be gaps in the walls of the bin to allow the air circulation necessary for decomposition to occur. The bin should be four feet square or larger and located in a shaded place. It will eventually reach a height at least equal to its width as organic materials are added in layers. As the heap grows in height, heat builds up in the layers of decaying matter and speeds the decomposition of the material.

If you cannot accommodate the suggested bin size in your garden, smaller ones may be constructed, though it is preferable with these smaller heaps to incorporate some organic material into the soil rather than wait for the whole heap to decompose. In this way the nitrogen used by the bacteria in the decomposition process comes from the matter itself and not from the soil. Thus, if undecomposed organic material is incorporated into the soil, allow a little extra nitrogen when applying fertilizers. If you prefer buying an already constructed bin, several small ones have been introduced onto the market recently. You can also use such readily acquired items as large plastic garbage cans if space is very limited. If you have sufficient room consider the ideal—two small compost bins: while one holds maturing compost, the other is being filled with fresh organic matter.

Include certain kitchen waste materials in the compost heap—coffee grounds, egg shells, skins and cores from fruits, vegetable peelings, etc.—plus garden refuse such as grass clippings and leaves. Do not include matter such as cabbage stalks, which take a long time to decompose, or meat because of its objectionable odor when it is decomposing. The materials should always be broken up into small pieces before adding them to the pile.

Place all materials in layers about four inches thick. Add dung in layers of the same thickness, if possible, as it will speed the decomposition process. If dung is not available, use a proprietary formula or sulphate of ammonia in the proportion of one-half an ounce to a square yard of soil and cover each four-inch layer with two inches of this soil. You may, if you wish, add this alternately with lime. If grass clippings are used, place them in with a bulkier material to allow air to circulate. Firm down after the addition of each layer of material. Continue building the heap until it is at least four feet high.

In dry weather, water the heap every week and turn it after four weeks; in cooler weather regions turn every six weeks. The heap should be watered after each turning and should be covered with a two-inch layer of soil. The compost will be ready for use after about three months, or as soon as it is a crumbly, brownish or blackish substance and each of the original ingredients is no longer recognizable.

TOOLS

Never buy tools which are not well made and comfortable to handle. The construction should be checked carefully before purchase. Smooth, close-grained handles are a must. The tools needed for maintenance of a small- or moderate-sized garden are a spade, digging fork, trowel, rake, hoe, measuring stick and hose. To this basic list add a cultivator, hand fork, small sprayer and wheelbarrow. With these, you are equipped to handle most operations in the garden.

Spade If your budget allows, buy a stainless-steel spade. It will be easier to clean and is more efficient in cutting through the soil. Make certain that the wooden handle of the spade is of a comfortable length and that the blade has a square edge. Pay special note to the point at

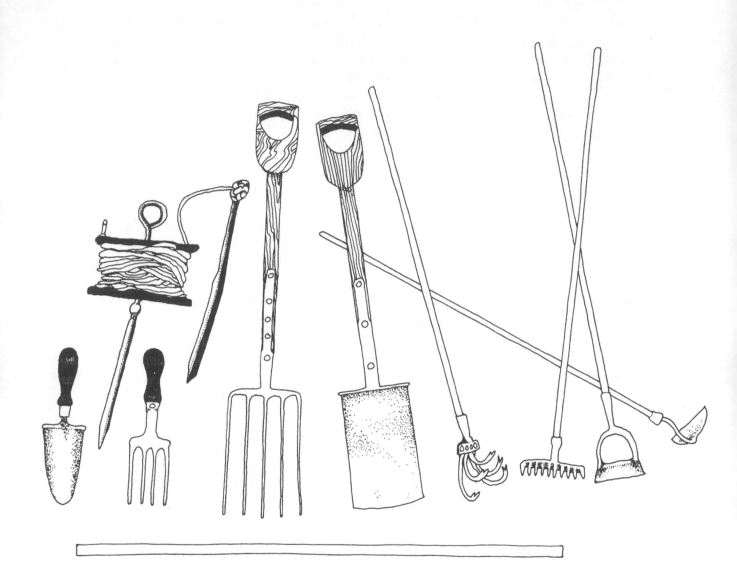

yard stick

garden line & reel   digging fork   spade   cultivator   rake   dutch hoe

which the handle joins the blade of the spade to make sure that the handle could be easily replaced should it break. I still cannot use a long-handled spade with any comfort and prefer a "D" handle. It is shorter and ends in a "D" shape which can be gripped easily and managed with ease.

Digging Fork As with the spade, be sure you purchase a fork which feels comfortable in the hand. The wooden shaft should be smooth to avoid splinters in the hand and the prongs should join the handle securely. The fork is essential for many operations such as turning the compost heap, preparing the ground after each harvest and loosening compacted soil.

Trowel Needed for transplanting, the trowel must fit the hand comfortably. Make sure that the blade is not too narrow. Frequently the blade is attached to the handle by a spike which has been driven up into the handle. These types of trowels can work loose easily. Be certain the attachment point between the blade and handle is secure.

Rake Because it is used to break up the large lumps after digging, to level the soil and to create a good tilth, the teeth of the rake should not be too close together or debris will catch in between, necessitating repeated removal. The teeth should also be at least three inches long. Often there is a weak spot in the rake when the bar which attaches the teeth to the handle is a separate piece of metal. It is better to have both teeth and attachment in one piece.

Measuring Stick The measuring stick is an important tool which is very often overlooked. You may use any straight piece of wood four to five feet long and mark it in inches on one side and feet and six-inch intervals on the other. This stick will be a help when measuring the distance between rows and between plants in the rows. Many yardsticks are given away by commercial firms. Attach one of these to a stronger piece of straight-edged wood and you have a tool which should last for several years.

Hoe There are several types of hoes on the market. I prefer the Dutch hoe for weeding. It is used by working backwards, slicing under the surface of the soil to cut down the weeds. This leaves the surface of the ground clean and free of footmarks. Again, whichever type of hoe you purchase, make sure that the point of attachment between the handle and the blade is secure.

Hose Purchase a good quality hose which can easily be used in all types of weather. Frequently, the less expensive plastic hoses are stiff in cold temperatures and thus awkward to use.

garden reel & line

Care of Tools Always clean tools after they are used. Oil the handles, especially when new. The entire surface of the tool should be well oiled over winter when its use is more infrequent. Some find that plunging the operative end of any tool in a box of sand mixed with oil during the winter will keep it in the best condition. And keep your tools stored in specifically designated places so they are always easy to locate.

With all the tools described and with any others you may see fit to add to your supply, always be certain to try them for "feel" before you buy. Shop around, ask your friends for recommendations and, finally, buy the very best you can afford.

PESTS

It is surprising how cleaning up debris and keeping weeds under control lessens the chance of attack by garden foes. There are some common-sense organic solutions to some of the most prevalent pest and disease problems. These ideas follow with each description. If the situation gets out of hand, however, you may decide to use chemical means to correct the problem. This is not to suggest that wholesale chemical warfare should be practiced. Remember that insecticides, herbicides and fungicides are meant to be killers and utmost care during their use is absolutely necessary. They can be extremely dangerous if used improperly on food crops. In all cases read the label carefully and follow its instructions explicitly, taking special note of the number of days required between use of the product and harvest of the crop. Each gardener must decide for himself his degree of reliance on chemical remedies in his garden.

Aphids These tiny insects are found in all colors, green being the most common. Aphids suck on plants and can pass along, in the process, a virus which weakens and distorts a plant. If aphids are not controlled quickly, a large colony can establish itself in very short order. A mild solution of soapy water or a garlic spray is sometimes successful in controlling aphids. Washing the aphids from the plant with a hard jet of cold water also helps. If these methods fail, use Malathion or a similar product for use on vegetables. Remember to spray when the insects are active. While aphids attack a wide range of crops, they seem partial to members of the cabbage family.

Leafhoppers These fast-moving little pests are green or brown in color. They feed on the undersides of leaves and cause a white spotted pattern which is seen on the upper surface. Again, cold sprays might help. Make sure that you hit the undersides of the leaf when spraying with water. If this method fails, use Malathion. Leafhoppers prefer beans, carrots, lettuce and potatoes.

White fly No garden is safe from attacks by this pest. White flies love tomatoes and beans and prefer the undersides of leaves, so you must check carefully for them. Daily spraying with a hard mist of cold water discourages them. If they persist, try a soapy water spray. As a last resort, hit them with Malathion. It will be necessary to spray every week or 10 days as they are fast breeders. They should not be left uncontrolled as they weaken plants considerably by sucking the sap.

Red spider Tomatoes, beans, melons, peppers and squash are all favorites of this pest. After attack, a yellow spotting on the leaf occurs. This spotting turns more vivid as the webs they build strangle the flow of food to the leaves. The leaves start to turn up at the edges and feel dry to the touch. Remove severely attacked leaves and spray the remaining with cold water. If you are experiencing a heavy infestation, spray with Malathion.

Cabbage worm and cabbage looper The former keeps his body flat, while the latter loops as he wanders on your plants. The best natural control is removal by hand. A new type of control is called *Bacillus thuringiensis.* This bacterium is safe for man but will kill the pest. It is purchased in a liquid form and applied to the heads of the cabbage before they are totally formed. Sevin is yet another product which will control this pest.

Beetles The Colorado potato beetle, bean beetle, Mexican bean beetle, flea and blister beetle all feed at night and are difficult to spot. If you see them, squash them. Clean debris where they can hide and use Sevin or Rotenone. The larger black ground beetles should not be killed, as they are carnivorous and feed on many garden pests.

Leaf miners If you happen to notice a series of tunnels on the leaves of your plants, sometimes in circles and sometimes in wriggly lines, the leaf miner is surely at work. If you check the plants frequently, you may be able to squash this pest in his tunnel. Always remove badly infected leaves. Rotenone will keep this pest under control.

Corn earworms Holes bored into ears of corn is the sign of this garden pest. One attack will occur in June or July, another in August. The pest is about one and a half inches long and is green or brown in color. Prevent attacks by dusting with Sevin as soon as the silks appear, repeating often until the silks turn brown.

Cutworms One morning you might go out into the garden and discover several of the stems of your tomatoes, cabbages, peppers, beans or corn eaten right through! If you dig up the roots you will see that they too have been nibbled. Cutworms at work! Apply a band of Sevin along the rows. This should control the problem. I know of no non-chemical method of stopping these pests.

Wireworms More prevalent in the western states, these pests puncture the stems, roots and tubers of plants. Especially hard on root crops, such as turnips, carrots and potatoes, they can weaken an entire plot of these vegetables in a very short time. Ask your nurseryman to recommend a chemical control. If invaded, place carrots as bait near the other crops.

Slugs and snails These two pests love to feed on tender growing plants. Look for snails in dark niches, under the foliage of low-growing plants and at the bottoms of containers. Piles of decaying plant material make them a lovely home so keeping the garden clean is a great help in controlling them. There are many methods of slug and snail control. Some people suggest setting out bowls of beer; the snails are attracted to it, then drown. Because they are nocturnal pests, they can be attracted to areas by putting out shingles, cabbage leaves or plant refuse and in the morning they will be found hovering about this debris. Scoop them up and drop them into soapy water or give them a good sprinkling of salt. Probably one of the best ways to protect your plants is to surround the planting beds with sand or cinders, which will keep the mollusks out. Even wood ashes can be used in this same manner. They keep snails away and at the same time nourish the soil. The most common method of combating these pests is slug and snail bait, which is sold commercially.

Earwigs While seldom causing serious damage to crops, these pests should be kept out of the garden. Place an empty flower pot upside down on a stake which stands about two feet above the ground. Fill it with straw. The earwigs will gather in the straw and then it can be destroyed.

To repeat, whenever you use a chemical control make sure it is cleared for use on the crop which is under attack. Always read labels carefully!

DISEASES

Conditions which promote growth of disease are lack of air circulation, unclean conditions and overcrowding of foliage (this latter creates a micro-climate in areas where humidity builds and fungus spores can develop). Good air circulation is essential as the passages of air through the foliage will dry the leaves of any surface moisture, thereby retarding spore growth. Judicious removal of unhealthy leaves will create a good line of defense against disease. Many seed firms have been working on disease-resistant vegetable varieties. Verticillium wilt has been largely eliminated through this method. The two remaining types of diseases which prevail are rusts and molds. Removal of affected leaves will help keep these conditions under control.

Where any signs of disease are present, avoid wetting the foliage of plants when watering because it may hasten the spread of the disease. In any case, overhead watering is not recommended for irrigating vegetables. If you have any serious problems in your garden, seek professional advice from your nurseryperson and follow it.

Downy mildew Looking like the mold which appears on stale food, this grey mold can be found on the leaves of cucumbers, cantaloupes, broccoli, cabbages and cauliflower. The first sign of this disease is a brown lesion surrounded by a light grey down on the undersides of the leaves. This shows on the surface of the leaf as a small circle of discoloration. If the attack is severe and simple removal of damaged leaves does not stop the situation, a commercial preparation such as sulphur dust will be required to save the crop.

Rust Small brown-orange pittings on the leaves is the mark of this disease. Thriving in damp muggy conditions, it can soon reduce the effective functioning of a plant. Pick off the diseased leaves and destroy them. Chemically, rust is controlled by the use of a fungicide spray, often the same one used to combat mildew.

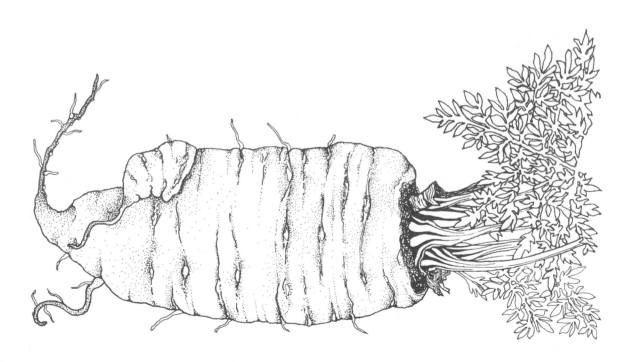

Specific Vegetables and Herbs

GLOBE ARTICHOKE
Cynara scolymus
Sun. Two seasons to maturity.
Sow seed mid-February indoors.
Plant April.
Grow in warmer areas only.

The globe artichoke originated from a wild thistle found in the western and central regions of the Mediterranean. This species was apparently carried some 2500 years ago into Egypt by wandering tribes. At this time the artichoke was also regarded as a great delicacy in Rome. After the fall of the Roman Empire, its popularity waned. There is no mention of it until the first record of the modern artichoke form, with a fleshy edible basal structure, was found in Naples around 1400. From there it was taken to Florence, where Catherine de Medici "discovered" and introduced it to the French as a gourmet delicacy.

While the English never developed a taste for them, artichokes were tremendously popular in France and Spain. The Spanish and French settlers took the artichoke with them to the colonies and, to this day, the areas which grow the largest crops are Louisiana, settled by the French and the central coast of California, settled by the Spanish.

The artichoke must be grown in soil rich in humus and provided adequate moisture. Large quantities of dung or compost should be worked into the soil with an addition, if possible, of superphosphate. Double digging the area is also recommended. If such preliminary care is taken, a plant can produce up to 40 heads in a season.

Artichokes may be grown in cold areas but do demand winter protection. They should not be grown where winter frosts are common. Start seed indoors in mid-February in a four-inch pot of good garden soil. In four to six weeks they will be ready to be planted outdoors. This should be done no later than April.

However, growing artichoke from seed does not always produce the desired results as there is usually too much variation. Asexual propagation is much preferred. Plants may be obtained from a nursery and planted out in mid-February or March. Plant two to three feet apart in rows with a four-foot space between the rows. As you can see, the artichoke is not a "small garden" plant. If space is a problem and you still are anxious to grow them,

artichokes can be grown as container plants. Keep the plants well watered. At no time should they be allowed to become dry. Monthly application of a liquid fertilizer is advisable. The plants will benefit from a top dressing of dung or seaweed, if the latter is available.

The plants will produce buds the second season, which lasts from September until May. Plants should be replaced every three or four years, using the offshoots which the old plants provide. In February, remove the strongest side shoots from the best producing parent plants and, after removing the old plants from the ground, replace with the young shoots.

To those not familiar with the delicious treasure hidden in its heart, the artichoke may appear coarse and unappetizing. The buds are the edible parts of the plant. They should always be harvested before they start to open. When cutting, leave about three inches of the stalk at the bottom of the bud.

Artichokes are not generally attacked by pests. There is a chance you may find aphids or an earwig or two in the bud. However, these pests seldom harm the bud itself. A thorough cleansing with acidulated water in the kitchen is preferable to garden spraying.

ASPARAGUS
Asparagus officinalis
Sun. Two seasons to maturity.
In warm areas, plant January/February.
In cold areas, plant in spring as soon as ground
   is workable.

Asparagus is native to Europe, growing wild around the Mediterranean and in Asia Minor. It thrives along river banks, lake shores and close to the sea. It has long been used by man for food. The ancient Greeks believed it grew from a ram's horn sunk into the ground and the Romans were cultivating it in 200 B.C. There are records of the Romans freeze-drying it.

Asparagus is a perennial and once established in the garden can produce for up to 40 years. While most vegetable plants contain both male and female parts, the asparagus is unusual in that there are separate male and female plants. The male plants are more productive, and since they produce no seed and thus no seedlings germinate to crowd the beds, growing male plants is preferable. (To distinguish between the two, the female plants produce pretty red berries while the male plants do not.)

While asparagus can be raised from seed, it is recommended that plants be purchased from a nursery. It is best to order the plants in advance so that there is only a minimum delay between their arrival in the nursery and your planting them in the garden.

Because the asparagus bed is going to be a permanent part of the garden, it requires extensive preparation. Asparagus grows best in a loose loam containing a good supply of organic matter. Dig a trench 10 feet deep and 12 inches wide. Fork a large amount of compost, dung, peat moss or other organic matter in the bottom of the trench. Form a ridge of soil along the base of the trench about four inches high. Set your plants 18 inches apart on this ridge, spreading the roots well. Cover the plants with two inches of soil. As they grow, gradually fill in the trench. Should you wish to have a double row of plants, dig the trench three inches wider, form two ridges and make two rows of plants, alternating the plants so there is the maximum distance possible between them.

Plant in the early spring. In areas where winters are cold, plant as soon as the ground can be worked and in other areas in January or February. Provide the beds with water throughout the year and always keep them clear of weeds. Do not harvest any spears until the second year, allowing the plants to become well established, and always leave some spears so that food can be produced by them and transferred to the roots for the next year's production. The best thing to do is cut only 10 days in the first year of harvesting, and then gradually increase the harvest time in subsequent seasons as the plants get larger. Cutting of the spears is best done with an asparagus knife. It has a "V" in the blade which slices off the spears below ground. When harvesting, also be careful not to damage developing spears. At the end of each season, remove and discard the dead tops of the plants.

If at all possible, cover the beds with dung during the winter to protect from the cold. Apply a 10-10-10 fertilizer in the spring as soon as growth has started, and again after harvesting.

As the seasons pass, mark any blank spaces in your asparagus bed and replace the following year. Once in full production, the plants should produce for many a year. And if you don't have the space to raise a large crop of asparagus, a couple of plants in a small garden will provide a delicious, special treat each spring.

BEAN

Phaseolus vulgaris—snap bean. Sun.
Bush, 50 days to maturity; pole, 65 days.
Warm areas, sow February/March; cold,
    April/May.
Phaseolus limensis— lima bean. Sun.
Bush, 65-70 days to maturity; pole, 85 days.
Warm areas, sow March/April; cold, May/June.

The word bean, like vegetable, has no specific meaning in terms of plant identification. It refers to the seeds of many different plants. The Indians of Central America carried the common bean, such as navy, red kidney, pinto, string or snap and the lima bean into South and North America. From there, the early explorers took them back across the Atlantic to Europe. The Indians ordinarily planted climbing beans along with maize. The maize, or corn, is high in starch and the beans high in protein. Combined in succotash (an Indian invention), they met most of the nutritional requirements of those tribes to which meat was rarely available.

The botanical names of common beans are: lima bean, *Phaseolus limensis;* string bean or wax bean, *Phaseolus vulgaris;* soybean, *Glycine hispida;* asparagus bean, *Delichos sesquipedalis.* Not generally grown but worth consideration for the home garden is the scarlet runner bean, *Phaseolus multiflorus.* Once the basic requirements of growing beans are understood, there should be no problems in realizing large crops of this nutritional food.

Snap beans are available in two forms, bush and pole. Snap beans mature in 50 days in full season when grown as bushes and in 65 days when grown on poles. Lima beans, when grown as bushes, mature in about 70 days; pole types in 85 days. Pole beans will out produce bush types by a wide margin and are, therefore, preferable for home gardens, especially where space is limited.

All beans require warm soil in which to germinate. Do not sow seeds until the spring is advanced enough for the nights to be completely frost free. The seeds can be sown in a sheltered location and planted out later, thereby advancing the growing season somewhat. If you decide to do this remember that beans may be damaged if their roots are disturbed and should be started only in peat pots which can be thrust directly into the soil after germination has taken place. The soil should be well cultivated before planting and frequent

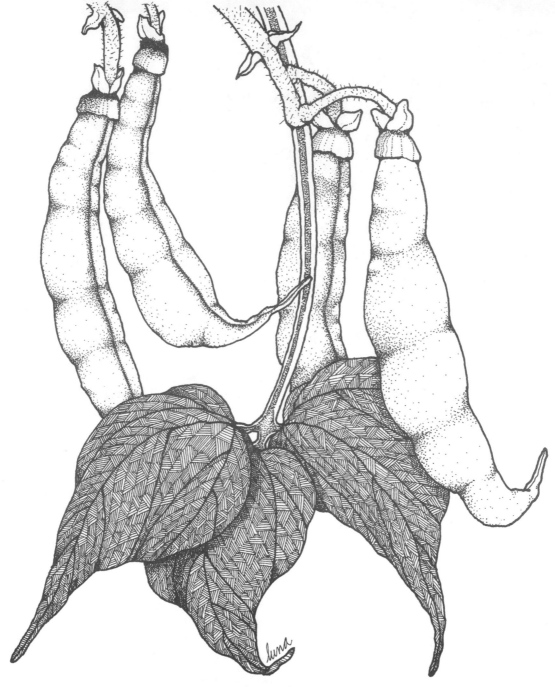

shallow cultivations should be made during the growing season. Constant moisture is a necessity but waterlogging the soil a danger.

Do not plant seeds at too great a depth and keep the surface soil in a crumbly condition during germination. Add some thin mulch to keep the surface broken, especially after watering, thereby allowing the seedlings to push their way easily through the soil to the surface.

When sowing seeds in place, plant the bush type one to one and a half inches deep, four inches apart. For pole type form either a tripod or construct a framework of wood or bamboo with a network of string upon which the beans will climb. Place six beans in the soil, at a depth of one to one and a half inches, at the foot of each string or pole. When the beans have reached a height of six inches remove the weakest, leaving three or four remaining. When positioning the pole for the climbing type, make sure the structure does not obstruct the sun.

As pole beans produce for a long period of time, they will require feeding during the growing season. An application of fertilizer every three weeks is advised after plants have made one foot of growth. Beans must be picked constantly and not be allowed to ripen on the vine or the plant will stop producing. Beans are generally not attacked by pests.

BEET
Beta vulgaris
Sun/light shade. 55-65 days to maturity.
In warm areas, sow January/April; again
   September/January.
In cold areas, sow April and September.

Our familiar garden beet developed from a thin-rooted perennial plant indigenous to the coastal regions of many countries. It is found in Denmark and England, around the Mediterranean and east to India. Over the years it developed into different forms which include sugar beet, manzel wurzel and chard.

Beets of the type which produce large fleshy edible roots were unknown before the Christian era. The ancients used the roots solely for medicinal purposes. The first recipes for cooking the root of *Beta vulgaris* were conceived by second- and third-century Romans.

63

The red beet, with a fat turnip-like root, was first described in a German work dated 1558. The plant was a rarity at that time in northern Europe. It was called a Roman beet, indicating its Italian origins. Until the 1800's only two kinds, red and long red, were listed by English seedmen. In 1806 only one variety was listed in seed catalogues in the United States. However, by 1828, four kinds of beet were available. Colors of garden beet varieties range from extremely dark purple red, to bright vermilion, to white.

The beet is a hardy crop. Native to coastlines, it thrives in areas where cool summer temperatures prevail. Hence, the seeds should be planted to reach maturity before the onset of hot summer weather. Seeds come in clusters. It is necessary to soak them in water, allow to dry slightly and separate them before sowing. If this process is neglected, the seed will germinate in groups of two or three plants.

Soil should be prepared the autumn prior to sowing. Sandy soil which is high in humus is ideal. Enrich the soil well with organic material, dig in thoroughly and leave fallow until the following spring. As soon as the ground can be worked, cultivate the soil lightly to achieve the finest tilth possible.

Sow the seed thinly in drills one and a quarter to one and a half inches deep, spacing 12 inches apart. Seeds will germinate erratically, seven to 10 days apart. Water the seedlings well and keep the area weed free. Sixty-five days after sowing, the beets should be ready to be pulled. A second sowing can be made 50 days before the first frost is expected. The plants can tolerate a certain amount of frost but nothing severe or prolonged. If frosts arrive prior to the estimated time, lift the beets and store them indoors in a little dry soil or sand. If you find it necessary to lift the beets early remove their green tops, which are edible.

If beets are cultivated in clay soil, expect a shorter growing season. Pull as soon as they are ready or the beets will be woody.

The maggots of the beet fly, a pest which may appear early in the growing season, can infect the leaves of the plant. It is best simply to remove the leaves which have been damaged or crush the maggot while it is inside the leaf.

65

BROCCOLI
Brassica oleracea var. *italica*
CAULIFLOWER
Brassica oleracea var. *botrytis*
Sun/light shade. 80-120 days to maturity
   from seed, 60-70 from plants.
Warm areas, sow early spring and late summer.
Cold areas, sow May/June.

While most people perceive a distinct difference between cauliflower and broccoli, botanically they are very similar. Both plants are derived from the same origin and the mass of immature flower heads. Cauliflower is a white-headed plant (created by blanching), while broccoli is green-headed.

Both plants are susceptible to temperature. The cauliflower does not like temperatures above 75° to 80°F and will not tolerate temperatures that fall below 30°F. In areas where winter temperatures are mild it can be grown as a winter crop. In other areas it can be grown as a spring or fall crop. Allow from 80 to 120 days for maturity from seed and 60 to 70 from planting the seedlings. In some regions in order to get a crop before the summer temperatures begin to be consistently above 75°, it may be necessary to start the seed indoors, planting out as soon as the danger of frost has past. For an autumn crop, count back the days from the first severe frost. If you can count on 60 or more days when the temperature averages will be 75°F or below, then you may plant the seedlings in late summer.

Broccoli will stand lower winter temperatures than cauliflower by about five to 10 degrees, and broccoli seedlings will stand the higher temperatures of summer. Thus it is possible to obtain both crops in many regions and in some a succession of these two fine vegetables. Neither broccoli nor cauliflower when mature can tolerate warm summer temperatures. For this reason, in the United States these two crops are commercially grown in coastal areas. The use of small frames or cloches allows earlier planting in the spring and harvesting prior to the heat of summer. It will also hasten the maturing of the plant in areas where the temperature is around the 30°F mark.

For an early summer crop of cauliflower the seed can be started indoors or in a frame six weeks before the last frost. Some latitude can be allowed as the plants will stand a few

degrees of frost. Sow seed thinly one-half inch deep. When seedlings are two to three inches tall prick them out into individual small pots. When frost danger has past plant seedlings 18 inches apart in rows two to three feet apart. Plant deeply into soil, even if this means covering several inches of stem below the leaves.

For a fall crop sow cauliflower seeds in May or June directly in the garden. Sow three or four seeds together one-half inch deep and space the groupings 18 inches apart. Remove all but the strongest plant in each group when a few inches high. Where a winter crop can be grown sow the seed in late summer in this same manner. In cases where the number of plants is not large, I recommend purchasing the seedlings from a nursery.

The plants like a pH of around 6.0 to 7.0. Never plant cauliflower (or broccoli) on ground which has just produced a crop of another cabbage. If the soil is a little on the acid side, add a dressing of lime prior to planting. Good rich loams are the best and compost should be incorporated into the soil prior to planting.

Fertilize cauliflower every six weeks during the growing season. Apply a 10-10-10 mixture along the rows, about one-quarter pound to every five feet of row. Make sure to water in well. Cultivation of the ground should be avoided as the roots of the cauliflower are close to the surface. When the head of the plant develops into the typical form, bend a leaf over the developing head to start the blanching. This process will take a few days in warm weather and longer in cooler weather. Some people go to elaborate methods to keep sunlight from the heads, but the breaking of leaves over the head is normally effective enough. If in doubt, tie the leaves together.

Broccoli is treated in much the same way as cauliflower. The seed is sown in the same way either indoors or out and the soil and fertilizer requirements are the same. It does like very firm ground and the soil, if cultivated, should be trampled down and made hard before setting out plants. As broccoli is a little hardier than cauliflower, more latitude can be allowed for the fall crop. Frequently the first frost is followed by a period of good weather and broccoli can withstand this first frost. In either case reduce watering to make the plants more resistant to the cold. The sap of the plant can be regarded as an antifreeze agent and the more it is diluted with water the less effective it becomes. (This rule applies to all plants and should be borne in mind when getting garden plants ready for the winter.)

Remember with broccoli that after the main head has been harvested the side branches will grow out and provide another picking some weeks later. Remove the plants only after all potential crops have been harvested or the frost has hit. The stumps of these cabbage plants are hard to break down in the compost pile unless a shredder is available.

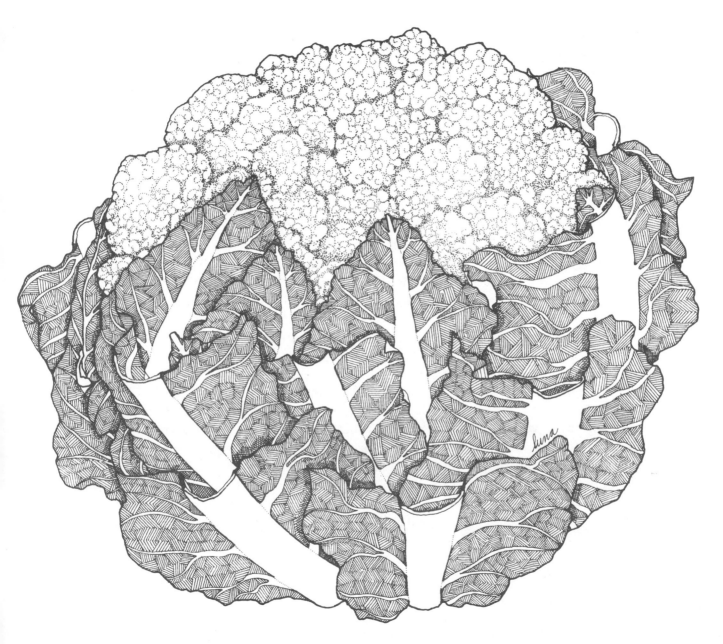

69

Be on watch against slugs and snails. Cutworms can be prevented by placing a paper cup with the bottom removed over each seedling. Watch for caterpillars during the growing season and remove by hand.

Many people may be intimidated by these temperature-sensitive plants. The wide spacing they require may seem to be a drawback for a small garden, but it is possible to grow lettuce, bush beans or other quickly maturing crops between the rows. This factor, combined with the high price of these vegetables in the market, makes their cultivation well worthwhile.

BRUSSELS SPROUT
Brassica oleracea var. *bullata gemmifera*
Sun. 120 days to maturity from seed,
   90 days from plants.
In mild climates, sow April, plant June;
   successive sowings.
In cold areas, sow July.

Brussels sprouts are so named because the plant is supposed to have been grown in the vicinity of Brussels since prehistoric times. While the vegetable developed there and attained importance in that region, it has only been known commonly in other areas for the last 400 years, a short time in terms of plant history. The first rough description of Brussels sprouts was made in 1587 and was evidently well circulated because by the 17th century botanists in Europe were writing about the plant without ever having seen it! Not until 1800 were Brussels sprouts commonly known in France. By 1850 they were under cultivation in England, where they have remained in high favor, probably due to the ideal growing conditions. Known in the United States since the 1800's, the largest crops are grown on Long Island, New York, and along the California coast.

The plant is really a tall-stemmed cabbage in which many tiny heads or "sprouts" form along the stem at the base of the leaves at the top of a short stalk, instead of forming one large head.

Brussels sprouts need a long cool growing season; they are not plants for hot regions of the country. But they are comparatively hardy and have been harvested at times when the frost had to be shaken from the plants.

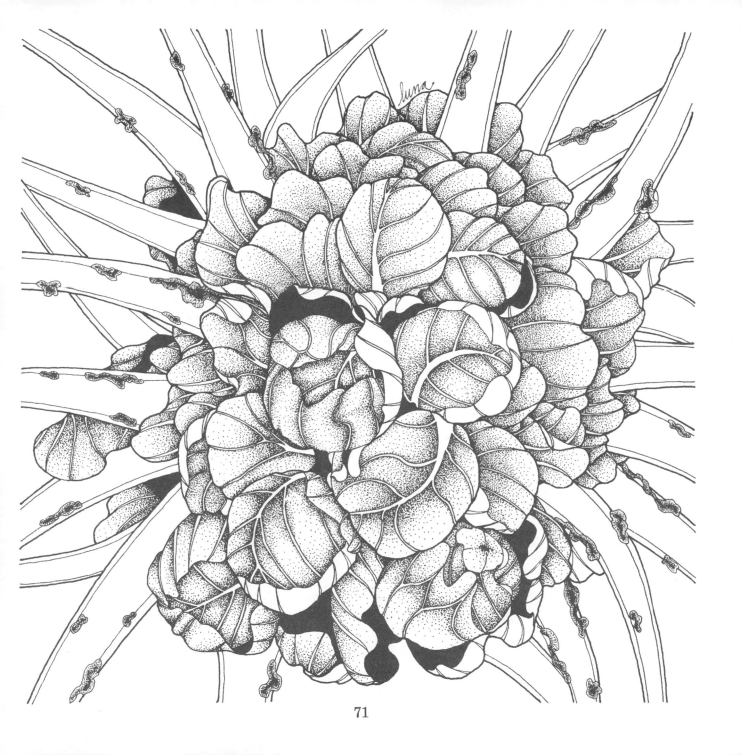

71

Brussels sprouts take a total growing time of 120 days. The seeds should be sown in a seedbed in July. In four to six weeks the seedlings will have reached a height of four to six inches and should be transplanted into the regular beds.

Rich sandy loam is the ideal soil for this crop. The soil should be prepared with an all-purpose fertilizer some weeks before planting. A moderate application of nitrate will enhance the color of the sprouts. Space the plants two and a half feet apart with three feet between the rows. Keep them well watered and the soil firm. When the buds begin to develop, the leaves on the stems should be removed in order to expose the buds. As the plants reach a height of two and a half to three feet, the growing tip may be removed to hasten the bud's development, though this is not essential.

A fast-maturing crop, such as lettuce, may be planted between the plants. The first sprouts should be ready to harvest in 90 days and the lower buds should be harvested first. Six plants will produce enough sprouts for several meals for a family of four.

In coastal regions or areas where the summer temperatures do not go above 75° to 80°F, it is possible to grow a succession of crops. Sow seed in April, transplant in mid-June, harvest in mid-September. Follow the first sowing with a second in three weeks time and continue harvesting until November. Don't worry if the weather is showery during planting.

Never plant two successive cabbage crops in the same ground. In warmer areas, follow sprouts with beans, leafy greens or a root crop. In cooler areas, allow the ground to lie fallow and plant a crop, other than cabbage, the following spring.

The plants may be attacked by caterpillars, which should be removed. Aside from this, Brussels sprouts are generally free from pests and diseases.

CABBAGE
Brassica oleracea var. *capitata*
Sun. 100 days to maturity from seed, 60 from
    plants.
In warm areas, sow September; successive
    sowings.
In cold areas, sow March and August.

Wild cabbage is apparently indigenous to the eastern Mediterranean and Asia Minor as well as to southern England. The ancient Greeks and Romans are said to have spread its cultivation north, while the Celts, who invaded much of the then-known world between the eighth and second centuries B.C., spread it south and to the Far East. The Celtic *cap* or *kap*, meaning head, developed into the German *kohl*, French *caboche*, Hindi *kopi* and, of course, the English cabbage. The wild cabbage of ancient times was non-headed; under domestication it developed into the hard-headed varieties we know today.

Cabbage does not thrive in hot weather and therefore should be planted to mature before the summer months arrive. Most varieties average 100 days to maturity from seed or 60 days from the setting out of seedlings. Should you wish to raise your crop from seed, start it in a flat or small seedbed. Thinly sow the seed in drills one-half inch deep three to four inches apart. When the stems are about the size of a thin pencil, they are ready to transplant. Select only the strongest seedlings for planting out and arrange them 18 inches apart in rows that are three feet apart. While seed is easy to raise, it is better to buy a few plants at a time from a nursery and have a succession of harvestings.

As cabbage is a leaf crop, it requires a large amount of food and moisture during the growing season. Before planting the ground should be well cultivated, incorporating a generous amount of organic matter. Cabbage also needs a heavy dose of nitrogen. Apply a 14-10-10 fertilizer to the soil a few days before planting and again when the plants have started to produce some growth (about three or four weeks after setting out).

In warm areas it is possible to set the plants out in the late summer and harvest in the early spring. The plants are very hardy and will take the cold weather in their stride. Make sure you plant the cabbage after the last of the hot summer weather has passed. In colder

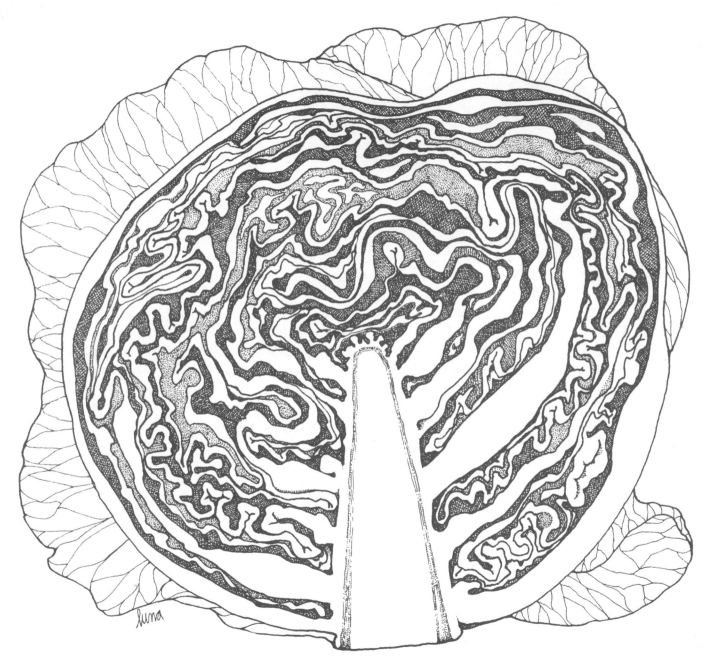

74

areas allow at least three weeks before the cold hard frosts arrive so the plants will be established enough to survive the rigors of winter.

Cabbage is susceptible to a disease called yellows. However, there are many varieties available which have been developed to resist this disease. Check with your nursery regarding information on these varieties. Slugs and snails are partial to cabbage. They can be picked off by hand, as can another frequenter of this crop, caterpillars. Keeping weeds under control and good garden hygiene should help in detering these pests.

Napa or Chinese cabbage would also make a good addition to your garden. These cylindrical-headed cabbages do not like extreme heat, which causes them to bolt. Sow seed early to harvest before the heat of summer, or sow in July. From seed to maturity is about 60 days. Plant the seeds, which are rather large, four inches apart in one-half-inch-deep drills with one to one and one-half feet between rows. Thin to eight inches apart when seedlings are up. Always provide adequate moisture, and some shade if the sun turns very hot. You will need to tie lengths of twine around the body of the cabbage when it begins "hearting." This will keep the head firm and growing compactly.

CARDOON
Cynara Cardunculus
Sun. 150 days to maturity.
In warm areas, sow September through
    March/April.
In cold areas, sow in spring after all danger
    of frost.

The cardoon, a form of artichoke, was grown in Sicily, Greece and ancient Carthage before the Christian era. It was one of the most popular garden plants in second-century Rome, bringing a higher market price than any other at the time. It was used cooked as greens, and raw in salad. Like the artichoke, the cardoon resembles an enormous thistle plant. It had been grown all over the Mediterranean for centuries before it was introduced into England in the mid-1650's. It was first grown in America in the 18th century. In the United States, it is cultivated primarily in the southern states. Cardoon is a vegetable which is generally blanched, much in the same manner as celery.

Planting is done in the spring. Dig a trench one foot deep. Spread and rake the bottom

with a maximum amount of compost or manure. Sow groups of three or four seeds spaced 20 inches apart with three feet between the rows. As the seeds are frequently eaten by mice, a cover placed over the trench will insure protection until the seeds have germinated. As soon as germination has started, thin out the plants, leaving the strongest plant in each grouping. During the growing season keep the plants well watered and weed free. By late summer the plants will have reached a height of three or more feet.

At this point the blanching process begins. First, tie the leaves together. Next, wrap the stems in brown-paper strips, six inches wide. Start wrapping from the base of the plant and work up, ending at the base of the leaves. Then pack a two- to three-inch thickness of straw to a height of 18 inches from the base of the plant around the paper-wrapped stem. Tie securely with string. Fill in the trench with the excavated soil. The blanching process will begin on the protected portion of the plants. After six weeks dig up the plants and store them, without removing either the paper or the straw, until you wish to use them.

Cardoon is not bothered by either pests or diseases. Because it is a large plant when mature, it should be grown only where adequate garden space is available.

CARROT
Daucus Carota var. *sativa*
Sun. 70 days to maturity, depending on
   variety.
In warm areas, sow year round.
In cold areas, sow March/April through
   mid-September.

In that part of the world which used to be known as Asia Minor, there grows a purple carrot and in Japan there is a variety which reaches a length of three feet. Our common carrot, though, is called the Mediterranean type, because it has long been grown in that region and was probably developed there from varieties carried from the East. The carrot was certainly cultivated in the Mediterranean area before the Christian era, but was not important as a food until much later.

By the 13th century, carrots were being grown in fields, orchards, gardens and vineyards in Germany and France. At that time the plant was also known in China. Since it originated in the Middle East, we must assume that it was carried to various parts of the world by traders and migrating tribes. By the 16th century, Europe's botanists were describing many kinds, including red and purple in France and yellow and orange-red in England. About 1600 in England, carrots were grown as a farm crop as well as in gardens.

European voyagers took the carrot to America soon after the discovery of the New World. It was grown by the colonists of the first permanent English settlement at Jamestown, Virginia, in 1609. The American Indians became very partial to the carrot. In forays against the Iroquois in upper-state New York in 1779, General John Sullivan's forces discovered and destroyed stores of carrots.

Carrots are fairly hardy plants and can be grown with success in both warm and cool climates. They like a sandy loam soil that is well limed and kept light so as to allow the taproot to grow straight down. The soil should be well worked and high in humus. Fertilize with 5-10-10 formula two weeks after germination and again in three weeks.

In warm areas, seeds may be sown all year round. In cold climates, the first planting should be at the end of March or in April. Last sowings in cold areas should be in mid-September. Seed should be sown one-half inch deep in rows 12 inches apart, with about four seeds to each inch of the row. When sowing, mix in a little radish seed. The radishes will germinate first and mark the rows, as well as provide some extra food for the table. Thin the carrots to two inches apart when they are well up and use the thinnings in the kitchen. A second thinning should be done a few weeks later. The final spacing should leave the plants three to four inches apart. Lettuce may be planted between the rows for maximum ground use. Successive sowings of carrots can be made at three-week intervals.

Carrots are grouped into types according to size and shape. The Chantenay type is short to medium in size. It grows well in wet fall weather and in heavy soil. Sweet in flavor, it matures in 65 to 70 days to a length averaging six inches. The Nantes, because of its characteristic shape and high quality, is a superior carrot. It grows to a length of eight inches and is cylindrical in shape, the tip being almost as broad as the butt end. It is higher in sugar content than most other varieties and has a beautiful red-orange color. It matures in 70 days. The Oxheart type is a third longer than it is broad, tapering gradually toward the tip. It grows to a length of three inches and matures in 70 to 80 days. This type does well in heavy soil and is ideal for canning or freezing. The Finger type, a quick growing little carrot, matures in 60 to 68 days. Only about three and a half inches long, it is particularly well suited to shallow soils. It has very smooth skin, good color and is very tender.

Carrots are easily grown and may be used as appetizers, in salads, in main dishes and in desserts. A "must" in any home garden. Pests and diseases are not generally a problem.

CELERY
Apium graveolens
Sun/light shade. 85-100 days to maturity.
In warm areas, sow February-March indoors.
In cold areas, sow late March indoors,
    plant mid-May.

Wild celery grows in damp places in Mediterranean lands (where it probably originated), Asia Minor, the Caucasus and Europe. The Chinese wrote about celery in the fifth century A.D. The oldest written record in the West is in a ninth-century poem of French origin in which the medicinal virtues of the plant are extolled. When its garden culture began, in 16th-century Italy and northern Europe, the plant was still quite primitive and was used for medicinal purposes only.

Celery was first used in cooking as a seasoning. By the late 17th century it was sometimes eaten as a salad with an oil dressing. In the 18th century celery was being refined in order to eliminate some of its bitter flavor. Gardeners had discovered that the flavor was vastly improved by planting in late summer and maturing in the winter. They had, in fact, by the mid-18th century cultivated a great delicacy which was in demand all over Europe.

Celery is not an easy plant to grow; it demands a great deal of the gardener's attention. It is also a slow-growing plant which takes a minimum of 85 days to reach full maturity. Because growing celery plants from seed can be tedious, you may elect to purchase seedling plants at a nursery and forgo the germinating and transplanting steps. If you prefer starting from seed, sow in flats in February in the warmer areas of the country and in late March in the colder areas. Seeds can be started later in mild climates for late fall crops. Make sure that the soil is very fine and liberally supplied with humus. Sow seeds to a depth of 1/16 of an inch. Keep the flats in an area where the temperature is warm, about 55°F. When the seeds have germinated, prick the seedlings out into other flats. Plant them five inches apart and keep them well watered. About two weeks before plants are ready to be set out in final position, dig rows of 12- to 15-inch-deep, eight-inch-wide trenches spaced one foot apart. Be sure to incorporate a good amount of compost into the bottoms of the trenches. In

mid-May the young plants should be removed from the flats and planted eight inches apart in the prepared trenches.

When the plants are one foot high, begin the blanching process. This process removes the bitter taste, encourages the development of the heart and improves the appearance of the celery. First tie the stalks together loosely to prevent the soil from getting between them. Start piling earth around the plant up to the height of the leaves. This should be repeated when the plants are 18 inches high. The same results may be achieved by using newspaper rolled around and tied to the stalks. In fact, since the purpose is to prevent light from striking the stalks of the plant, any method which is easiest for you is acceptable. Most early varieties are "self-blanching," but they preclude this process only to a degree. The complete exclusion of light is necessary for the stalk to mature properly. Feed the plants with a 10-10-10 fertilizer every three weeks and water heavily. Harvest the celery when it is of a sufficient size by making a clean cut at the roots. A second sowing of seed may be made eight weeks after the first. This will assure a continuous crop.

In certain areas of the country, mildew may be a problem. At the first sign, remove any leaves so attacked. Celery fly is a more serious concern and must be treated with a spray developed to combat it, which you can obtain at your nursery. Slugs and snails should be removed.

CHARD
Beta vulgaris var. *Cicla*
Sun. 60-75 days to maturity.
In warm areas, sow February/March,
    October/November.
In cold areas, sow March/April.

Chard is a foliage beet which has been developed for its large fleshy leaf stalks and broad crisp leaf blades. It is one of the best potherbs for summer use, for it withstands hot weather better than most crops grown for use as greens. Although improved in size, compactness and edibility over ancient forms, the several types of chard grown now have been known for hundreds, some for thousands of years.

In the year 350 B.C., Aristotle wrote of red chard. He evidently told his successor in

83

the Peripatetic school, Theophrastus, about the delicious flavor of both the light and dark green varieties, for he, too, wrote on the subject. The Romans were very familiar with chard. We know that it was well established on the Iberian peninsula in the 13th century. In the 16th century a Swiss botanist described a yellow form, completing the list of types now known.

While chard is best grown as an annual, in some particularly mild areas it will overwinter and is, in these regions, thought of as a biennial. If you do grow it over for a crop the second year, make sure the seed or flower spike is removed even if it appears in the first growing season. There are several varieties of chard available for planting. They vary in color from greens to red and appear in assorted leaf shapes, some of which are very beautiful. If you are short on space in your garden, chard may be used as a productive ornamental or a decorative vegetable, whichever you choose!

Chard is a marvelous vegetable. The rib of the leaf can be cut out and cooked and served like asparagus. The blade of the leaf is cooked as any green vegetable. You will find chard to have a sturdier texture and more robust flavor than spinach, with which it is often compared.

Chard can tolerate temperatures as low as 24°F. In areas where such winter temperatures prevail, it is best to sow the seeds two weeks before the last frost is due. Where the winters are mild, a crop may be sown in October or November. Chard will withstand dry conditions but, naturally, the more moisture available, the better the production. As is the case with all leafy vegetables, a good supply of plant food will make for a more prolific harvest.

Sow the seeds in shallow drills and space them well apart. Plants may also be raised in flats and upon reaching five to six inches in height, can be transplanted into the ground eight to ten inches apart. If you have sown seeds in place, thin them out to this distance when the plants are of fair size, but before they touch. If more than one row is planted, keep rows 18 to 24 inches apart.

By midsummer the plants should be in full production. Be sure to cut on a regular basis to prevent the outer leaves from getting tough. Cut the leaves about one and a half inches above the ground to keep the plant producing well, and do not take too many leaves off or you will weaken the plant. Regular watering during the summer months is important to insure continuous leaf production. You can expect a minimum harvest of one pound of leaves per plant over a 90-day period.

Snails and slugs, which seem to relish tender leaves as much as we do, are the only pests to worry about.

COLLARD
Brassica oleracea var. *acephala*
Sun. 80 days to maturity.
In warm areas, sow August/September.
In cold areas, sow April/May.

Collards are, in effect, primitive cabbages. More highly developed forms, such as cauliflower, broccoli and head cabbage, have been produced only in the last 2,000 years. Collards are native to the eastern Mediterranean region or to Asia Minor but, because of constant shifting about by traders and migrating tribes, their exact place of origin is unknown.

The Greeks ate collards long before the Christian era. The Romans, too, grew a mild-flavored type with large leaves and stalks. The word collards is a corruption of *coleworts* or *colewyrts*, Anglo-Saxon terms meaning cabbage plants. During the time of their great conquests, the Romans carried collards to Britain and France. The first mention of collards in America was in 1669 but, because of their popularity in Europe, it is assumed they were introduced somewhat earlier.

Collards do not thrive in constant hot weather, a condition that will give the plant a strong undesirable flavor. Cool growing weather, fall frosts and mild winters impart a high sugar content and fine flavor. Collards are among the easiest of all vegetables to grow and, in recent years, nutritionists have sought to popularize this plant because of its unusually rich mineral and vitamin content. When the plant is young it resembles cabbage, each collard plant having a rosette of beautiful green-blue leaves. However, as the plant matures, it does not form a head of tightly compressed leaves as the cabbage does. Instead, its stems elongate, almost in a treelike fashion, eventually reaching two to four feet in height. Since each leaf is fully exposed to the sun, they become deep green and contain much more vitamin A and C than cabbage. The leaves can be eaten raw in salads or as a cooked vegetable.

Collards should be planted in full sun. The soil should be well drained and contain a good amount of organic material. In areas where winter temperatures never get below 25°F,

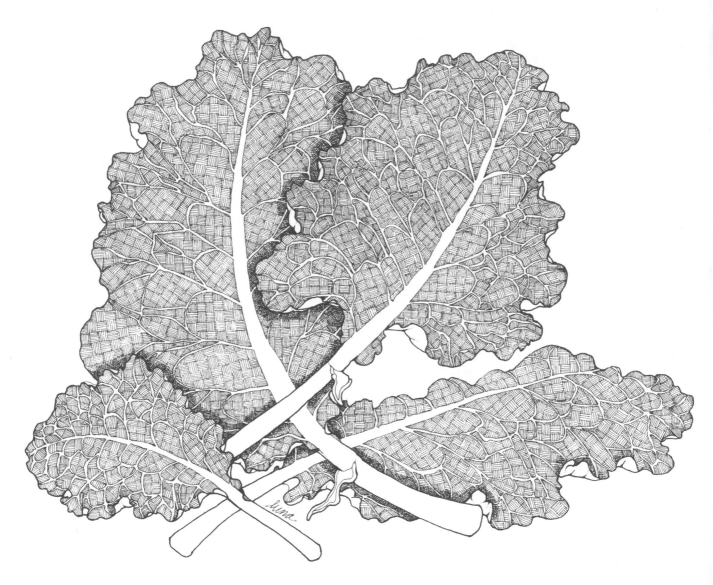

the seeds may be sown in the fall. If the winter temperatures do drop below this level, delay sowing until such temperatures no longer occur.

Sow the seed thinly in shallow drills, three feet apart. When the plants begin to come up they should be thinned until they stand some 24 inches apart in the rows. As with cauliflower and broccoli, the space between the rows may be used for beans, peas and salad crops, such as lettuce and radish.

Keep the soil moist during the growing season and fertilize with a 10-10-10 mixture every three or four weeks as the plants are growing. They will reach full maturity after 80 days. As soon as the production of side leaves slackens, remove the tops and then the stalks. A continuous supply may be maintained by successive sowings. As with other cabbage crops, no collards should be grown in ground that has been used for a cabbage crop in the preceding months.

The plants require protection from slugs and snails and from cabbage butterfly caterpillars, which should be removed and killed.

CORN
Zea Mays var. *rugosa*
Sun. 65-90 days to maturity.
In warm areas, sow February; successive
    sowings.
In cold areas, sow April; successive sowings.

In Anglo-Saxon, the word corn means a cereal crop of any kind—in Britain wheat, in Scotland and Ireland oats, in the Americas maize. Maize is the Indian word for corn, and this crop's first great period of development probably took place in the Andes region of southern Peru. When the tribes of this area migrated northward to Central and North America, they took supplies of maize with them. This parent grain, when planted in its new surroundings, hybridized with the wild indigenous forms and developed several new varieties. Before the white man reached America, most Indian tribes commonly grew maize as a staple. This maize, however, did not resemble the sweet corn of today.

There is a tremendous range of corn varieties. There are four-inch ears which grow on plants two and a half feet high, and there are eight-inch-long ears which grow on plants eight feet in height. Corn has a small yield in relation to the space it uses, so the decision to grow it will depend on available space.

Corn is a very adaptable crop, but grows best in warm temperatures in rich soil with good drainage. (Varieties have been developed which tolerate cooler temperatures.) The ground should be well fertilized in preparation for the growing of corn. For each 10 feet of row, use one-third to one-half pound of a fertilizer higher in phosphorus and potassium than in nitrogen. This should be spread on either side of the row about three inches away from the planted seeds. Plant seeds at a depth of two inches, five inches apart, leaving 30 to 36 inches between the rows. It is best to grow corn in short blocky rows for it to cross-pollinate successfully. When the seed has germinated, thin out to a distance of 12 inches between the plants. Water well during the growing season; deep watering is especially important after the tassels and silks appear. Fertilize when plants are 10 inches high and again at 24 inches high. Use the same kind and amount of fertilizer as in the original ground preparation.

Since there are early, mid-season and late varieties available you may follow up plantings with successive sowings every two or three weeks, ending with a variety which will take some frost. In this manner you will obtain the maximum use of the soil. Corn should be ready to harvest about three weeks after the silks appear. Carefully check a few ears by making a small opening in the husk so you can examine the kernels; they should squirt a milky substance when pressed with a fingernail.

The corn borer, a pest which can decimate your crop if not dealt with at the first sign of attack, can be kept under control by the use of sprays. Sevin is one product which is very effective. Simply follow the package directions. Watch for a first attack in June and one following in about two months. Corn earworms attack when the silk tassels appear. They go away when the tassels turn brown. During this period it is wise to dust every few days to keep this pest under control.

luna

CUCUMBER
Cucumis sativus
Sun (light shade in warm areas). 60 days to
    maturity.
In warm areas, sow March/April.
In cold areas, sow April/May.

The cucumber is probably native to the warm hills and valleys of northern India. The Romans used special methods to grow the cucumber out of season; Emperor Tiberius ate cucumbers daily, the year round. History records that Charlemagne grew them in his famous gardens in the ninth century. They were first grown in England in the 14th century. Columbus planted cucumbers in Haiti in the year 1494. In 1539, De Soto reported the Indians of Florida were growing cucumbers "better than those of Spain." Most of the distinct types grown today were known 400 years ago.

The plants are started from seed three weeks before the last frost is due. Sow two seeds one-half inch deep in a three- to four-inch pot. When the first growth appears remove the weaker of the two plants. Continue to grow the plants until the roots start showing through the drainage holes in the pot bottoms.

Cucumbers are planted on small hills six inches high and two feet across. They like sandy soil and full sun or light shade. Dig a hole five to six inches deep and fill with compost which is well mixed with soil. Replace the earth which was removed. You should then have a mound built up about six inches in height. Plant three young cucumbers across the top of the hill, leaving a space of one foot between the plants. The hills should be four feet apart in rows six feet apart. Train the plants to trail down the slopes of the hills.

Seed may be sown directly into the hills if the temperature permits and if all frost danger is past. Plant seeds in groups of three spaced one foot apart. When first growth appears, remove all but the strongest plant in each group and grow as described above. If you wish to avoid the first stage of growing seeds in pots or in place, young plants which are ready to set out may be purchased at the nursery.

Cucumbers can also be trained to grow on trellises, which is preferable for the small garden. Plant out young seedlings one foot apart in rows and tie three plants on a

luna

five-foot-wide trellis. One or two trellises of this size should provide ample fruit for an average family.

Plants must be kept moist throughout the growing season. Once the plants are well established, fertilize with a 10-10-10 mixture every three weeks. From time to time, top dress the roots with a mixture of well-rotted compost and topsoil, adding three inches at a time. Pinching back some of the shoots will result in better fruit. It is also necessary to remove the male flowers when they appear so that they do not pollinate the fruiting female blossoms. It will be easy to distinguish the male from the female blossoms, as the female will have the beginnings of a fruit forming behind it. Failing to remove the male blossom will result in bitter, large-seeded fruit. Two months after setting out, the first cucumbers will be ready for harvesting. Do not break fruit from the plant but cut cleanly. Always remove fruit before it becomes too large and old. The cucumbers will have better flavor and you avoid weakening the plant.

Spray the foliage with water in the early morning or late afternoon, when the sun is not on the leaves. This procedure will help keep down white fly, a common pest. Slugs and snails should, of course, be removed. Watch for cucumber beetle infestation and resort to chemical spray only if non-chemical methods are not effective. Saving seeds for next year's planting is not a good idea. The seeds will be weak, not produce a good crop and the resulting plants may be susceptible to a virus called cucumber mosaic, which causes mottling of the leaves and misshapen, discolored fruit.

EGGPLANT
Solanum Melongena var. *esculentum*
Sun. 90 days to maturity from plants.
Sow seed indoors mid-March;
    plant outdoors in June.

The eggplant is believed to have originated on the Indian subcontinent. The fruit is found in varying shapes and in colors ranging from dark purple to red, yellow and white. The numerous Arabic and North African names for the plant indicate it was carried into the Mediterranean area by traders early in the Middle Ages, and it is still widely grown in those

93

areas. Eggplant has been grown in China since the fifth century A.D. Fashionable ladies of the period used a dye made from the plant to stain their teeth. Introduced to America by the Spaniards, eggplant was grown in Brazil around the mid-1600's. However, it was rarely eaten until about 50 years ago. Up to that time it was thought of only as an ornamental. In the United States, the large pear-shaped purple type is preferred; a smaller eggplant with elongated fruit is grown in the Orient.

Native to warm climates, the eggplant requires a good deal of summer heat to produce quality fruit. It needs 90 nights of mid-50°F temperatures and the same number of days in which the temperature maintains an 80°F or higher level. In areas where short summers prevail it is wise to purchase the varieties of eggplant which mature 60 days after setting out.

Start seed indoors about mid-March. Sow two or three seeds in a small pot, using a sandy soil mix which has never been used to grow vegetables. Place the pots, six or eight should do, in a warm moist area. After the seedlings reach a height of four inches, remove all but the strongest plant in each pot. If you wish to avoid this first indoor stage of propagation, purchase young plants which are ready to be set out in the garden. These are available at nurseries and garden centers. Set the plants out in June in a warm sunny spot. Since eggplants require copious amounts of water, they should be planted in a shallow trench so the plants can be gently flooded when watered. Plant two feet apart in loose, fertile soil, leaving a distance of three feet between the rows. An application of 5-10-5 fertilizer is advised at planting time.

Each plant will produce four to six good-sized fruits. You may find it a good idea to pinch out some terminal growth and blossoms to prevent too many fruits from forming on each plant. When harvesting, be sure to cut the fruit from the stalk as pulling can cause damage to the plant. Harvest while the fruit is shiny. Since eggplant is a relative of the tomato and potato plants, it should never be grown in soil which has produced either of those crops the previous year. Watch for infestation by aphids or white fly and occasionally beetles. Verticillium wilt, a disease caused by organisms in the soil, can sometimes be the cause of failure with eggplant.

LEEK
Allium Porrum
Sun. 150 days to maturity from seed,
   80 from plants.
In warm areas, sow February/March.
In cold areas, sow April/May.

Leeks have been common all over Europe for as long as records have been kept on edible plants. The Romans thought the best leeks, which they called *porrum*, were grown in Egypt, where they had been cultivated since earliest times. The Emperor Nero reportedly was nicknamed Porrophagus because of his extraordinary appetite for leeks. He claimed they improved his voice.

Leeks can be cultivated to a length of 20 inches. However, a length of six to eight inches is more common. The stems are blanched, a process accomplished by withholding light, which keeps the stems from turning green. Leeks can be grown in a wide range of soils. However, the richer the soil, the better the leeks will fare. Therefore it is important to incorporate as much organic material as possible into the soil when preparing it for planting. Leeks must have adequate moisture during their growing season. If the soil is in good condition no extra fertilizer is required, but if it is not rich enough, a 7-10-7 formula fertilizer should be applied every month and well watered into the soil.

Leeks take 80 days to grow from transplanted seedlings and 150 days from seeds. It is recommended that seed be sown for transplanting in flats or beds. During the 70-day period when the seedlings are growing, the ground may be used for a fast-growing crop. In cold areas sow the seed as soon as the last frost is over. In areas where spring comes early, sow seed in February or March. Sow seeds thinly. When the seedlings reach a height of four to six inches, they are ready to be transplanted. Firm the ground well and make holes three inches in diameter, nine inches deep, spacing them eight inches apart. Drop the seedlings into the holes and water well. This deep planting blanches the stems and avoids the need for "earthing up." The plants will fill the holes as they grow, so that by the time they are ready to be harvested, the hole should be completely filled. Leeks are perhaps the only vegetable which can be grown without firming the seedlings.

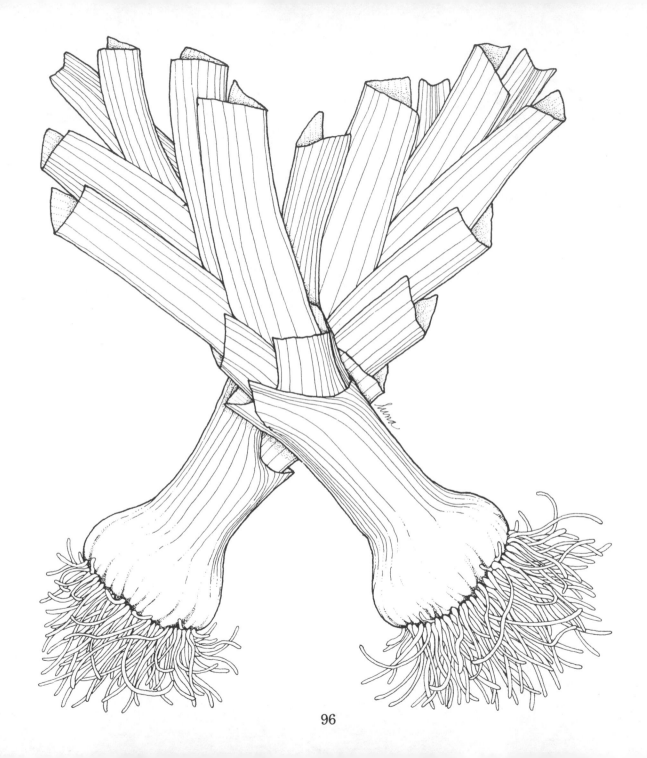

96

Leeks may also be planted without using the hole method for blanching, but this requires "earthing up," which is a more laborious procedure. Plant the seedlings in rows spacing the plants eight inches apart. During the growing season mound earth around the stems, thereby covering them and accomplishing the same result.

In areas where frosts do not occur until late in the year, a fall crop may be grown. Sow seeds 150 days before the first frost is expected. Leeks are comparatively hardy and are able to withstand some degree of frost as long as the plants are well established. Seedlings are more sensitive. In mild areas, such as in the southern states, a rotation of crops can be made.

The Welsh onion is a double misnomer. It is not an onion at all, but a leek, and its name is a corruption of the German *walsh*, meaning foreign, and has no reference to Wales. It never forms a bulb but, instead, grows long white scallions. This form of leek is most popular in the Orient.

Weeds must be kept under control. Rust may appear on the leaves. With good garden hygiene, however, leeks are an easy crop to grow.

LETTUCE
Lactuca sativa
Sun/shade. 45-90 days to maturity, depending
    on variety.
In warm areas, sow year round (shade in
    summer).
In cold areas, sow April to August; successive
    sowings.

Lettuce, the world's most popular salad ingredient, originated in Asia Minor, the trans-Caucasus, Iran and Turkistan. More than 2500 years ago it was cultivated in the royal gardens of Persia. Common garden lettuce has been grown in China since the fifth century. It was a favorite with the Romans around the beginning of the Christian era; writers of that period describe numerous types in cultivation. Firm-headed lettuce had become well developed in Europe by the 16th century. The oak-leaf and curled-leaf types, as well as the various colors now known, were all described in 16th and 17th century Europe.

Cos or romaine lettuce is formed of long leaves which approach the character of a head. Old records and its name indicate an Italian origin. Common in Italy since the Middle Ages, the romaine lettuce is said to have been taken to France in 1537 by Rabelais. It was

luna

98

Columbus who introduced lettuce into the New World, for its culture was reported on Isabela Island in the Bahamas in 1494. It was common in Haiti in 1565 and under cultivation in Brazil before 1650.

There are four principal types of lettuce available to us for home growing: leaf or loosehead, butterhead, head and romaine. Leaf or loosehead will mature in 45 days; the others take 70 to 90 days. Lettuce plants do not like frost! Sow under protection in the spring, indoors or in a frame. Set plants out, when large enough, after the danger of frost has passed. Ninety days before the first frost date, sow the last crop of all types except leaf, which may be sown 45 days before the first frost. In the warmest parts of the country, plant lettuce in the shade during the summer months. Lettuce does not like hot weather and will send up a flower spike if the temperature is too warm. In areas where the summer heat is excessive, select a variety which the seed company has suggested for growing under very warm conditions. Never let the plant suffer from lack of moisture, especially when the heads are beginning to develop. When watering, try not to get the leaves wet as this can cause them to burn if the sun strikes the leaf before it is dry.

Seed should be sown one-quarter inch deep in rows. If seedlings are grown for transplanting, make the rows six inches apart; if grown to mature in site, allow 12 inches between rows and thin out to 10 inches between plants. In a small garden, plant closer together and cut every other one before maturation to gain space and maximize crop yield. For continuous crops, make successive sowings every three weeks. Lettuce seed retains its viability for a number of years, but should not be sown when over five years old.

Lettuce demands a well-worked soil, high in humus content, that should never be allowed to dry out. It is important to keep the soil level and weed free. Fertilize with 5-10-10 every three weeks after the seedlings have reached a fair size, about three inches high or four inches across. When thinning the bed, remember that the leaves are edible at all times and the small leaves from the thinnings are very tender and delicious in salads. Lettuce lends itself to interplanting between such crops as peas, beans and cabbages.

In areas where lettuce can be grown year round, coastal regions of California and in some southern states where no frost occurs or where slight protection will shield from frost, allow a few extra days for maturing dates during the shorter sunlight periods of winter.

Slugs and snails are the worst pests. Aphids are also a nuisance. A spray cleared for use on food crops should be used only if the problem is severe.

OKRA
Hibiscus esculentus
Sun. 70 days to maturity.
In warm areas, sow February/March.
In cold areas, sow May/June.

Okra originated in Africa in an area which includes present-day Ethiopia and eastern Sudan. Due to the isolation of this region, little that is definite is known about the prehistoric origins and distribution of okra. We do know the plant was taken to North Africa and Arabia very early in history. From Arabia it was carried completely around the Mediterranean and eastward. Okra was cultivated in Egypt for many hundreds of years, having been brought there by Moslems from the east who conquered the Egyptians in the seventh century. One of the earliest accounts of okra was that of a Spanish Moor who visited Egypt in the year 1216. He described the plant in detail and stated that the pods were eaten while still young and tender.

Okra is a warm weather plant which requires a nighttime temperature of no less than 50° F. It also requires a large growing space, which must be taken into consideration before planting it in your garden. Seeds can be started indoors in the colder areas three weeks before the desired night temperatures become prevalent. Plant two seeds to a pot using the seed compost described on page 33. When the seeds germinate, plant out 18 inches apart with three feet between the rows. In areas where there are nighttime temperatures of 50°F in February and March, the seeds may be sown directly outdoors.

The ground should be well worked with humus and fertilizer before planting. Plant three seeds one-half inch deep in clumps 18 inches apart. Allow three feet between the rows. When the seeds have germinated, remove all but the strongest plants. Apply a dressing of a balanced fertilizer when the plants reach a height of 10 inches and repeat once more when the first flowers appear. The plants require a good supply of water during the growing season. Mulch or well-rotted compost or grass clippings will help retain the moisture. The flowers will be followed by seed pods, which should be harvested when four to five inches in length for best flavor.

If the pods are not kept picked, the plant will stop producing flowers and, consequently, pods. The time from seed sowing to pod production is about 10 weeks. Production will continue for a long time and the plant will eventually reach a height of four feet. It is seldom necessary to grow more than six plants for an average family's needs.

Okra is free from attack by pests and diseases but is vulnerable to those garden gourmets, the snail and the slug.

ONION
Allium Cepa
Sun. 160 days to maturity from seed,
    100-120 from sets.
In warm areas, sow February/March.
In cold areas, sow April/May.

There has been widespread cultivation of the onion since prehistoric times. The onion originated in middle Asia with secondary centers of development and distribution in western Asia and the Mediterranean. From drawings and inscriptions we know the ancient Egyptians used onions extensively. In fact, while in the wilderness, the Israelites longed for the onions, leeks and garlic they were used to eating during their years in Egypt. By the first century many onion varieties were known: long, round, strong, mild, yellow, white and red. The Spanish introduced the onion into the New World. Soon it was being cultivated in all parts of the Americas. The settlers grew them and, in turn, the Indians did.

Onions are very hardy plants. They will grow well in almost any soil but prefer rich light loam with good drainage, especially in the subsoil. They thrive in full sun and, unlike most other crops, can be grown in the same location year after year.

Seed takes 160 days to mature. In areas where winter is severe, the seeds should be sown in the spring as soon as the ground can be worked. This usually means April or May. In these areas the growing season can be quite short, sometimes less than 120 days. Therefore, the onions should be started indoors and set out as soon as the frosts are over.

In areas where winters are less severe, seeds may be planted in February and March. Work humus and fertilizer into the soil before planting. Sow seeds in drills one-half inch deep. Thin to four inches between plants and maintain 15 to 18 inches between the rows.

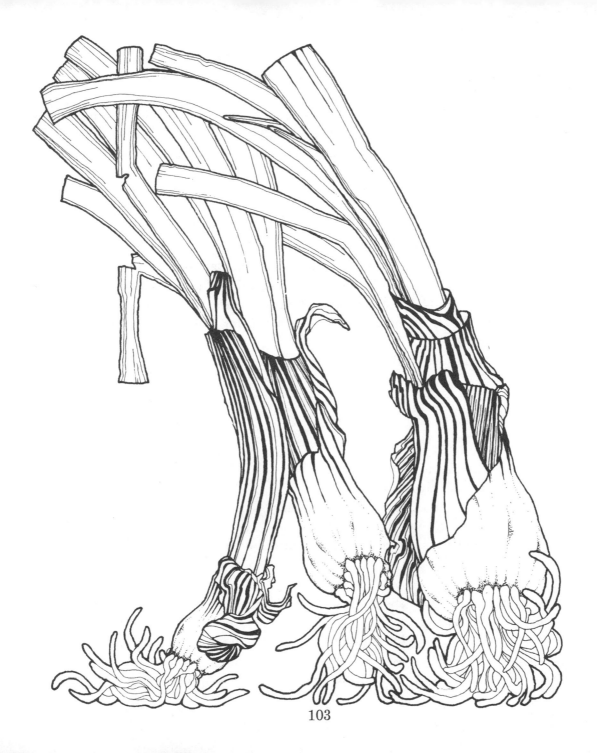

Make sure the seedlings are not planted too deep in the soil as the sun must get to the bulb for it to ripen. Water well and keep the area weed free. If the soil is not rich, feed every month with a 5-10-10 fertilizer.

During the last weeks of growth, the tops will start to yellow. This is normal. Break over the green growing parts so that the bulbs are exposed to a maximum amount of sun. This will help the ripening process. At this time no more watering should be done and discontinue feeding.

Raising onions from seed is a long and painstaking process, and for the small garden it is more practical to purchase "sets" available at most nurseries. These "sets" expedite cultivation tremendously and shorten the growing time to 100 to 120 days.

Onions grow their tops in cool weather and form bulbs in warm weather. The timing of bulb growth is controlled both by the temperature and the day length, in other words, the amount of daylight available. Onion varieties are classified by "long day" and "short day." In the summer, long-day plants are grown (14 to 16 hours of daylight); in the winter, short-day plants are grown (12 hours or less of light). After you harvest your onion crop, store it in a dry, airy place.

The uses of onions are so wide and the growing so comparatively easy, they should be part of every garden.

PARSNIP
Pastinaca sativa
Sun. 120 days to maturity.
In warm areas, sow January/February,
    July and August/September.
In cold areas, sow in spring as soon as ground
    is workable.

The parsnip is native to Europe and the eastern Mediterranean region. Emperor Tiberius had them imported each year from Germany, where they flourished along the Rhine. The modern parsnip was accurately illustrated in Germany in the year 1542. At that time it was the staple of Europe's lower classes, much as the potato is today. Parsnips were brought to the New World by the early settlers and the American Indians readily took up their

104

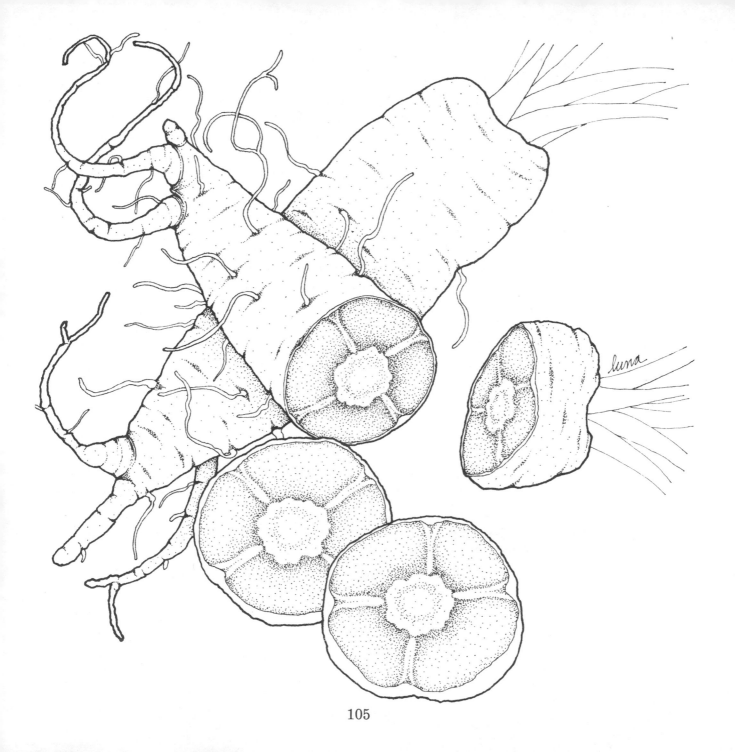

luna

cultivation. There are records of large Iroquois storehouses filled with parsnips being destroyed by the army in the wars with this tribe.

The plant is a hardy biennial, producing a root in the first year and a flower stalk in the second. In the garden, however, it is grown as an annual. Parsnips take 120 days to mature from seed and require substantial space for growing, so should not be attempted unless garden area is not restricted. In cold areas seed should be sown in the spring as soon as the ground can be cultivated. In warmer areas, seed may be sown in January or February and again in July and early fall. The crop can be left in the ground and harvested during the winter up to the spring. If you wish to try this and live in a cold region of the country, cover the area with a thick layer of straw to prevent the frost from freezing solid.

Parsnips grow best in deep, rich moist soil. The root is long, so the soil must be very well worked to a good depth, with compost added during the soil preparation. The seed should be sown thickly in drills one-half inch deep in rows spaced 18 to 24 inches apart. The soil should then be watered well and covered with a mulch of grass clippings or sifted compost to conserve the moisture and prevent the soil from caking. In this manner the seedlings can push their way up easily through the soil. When the seedlings are two inches high thin them to four to five inches apart. During the growing season apply a side dressing of 5-10-10 fertilizer along the rows once a month. Keep the area well watered and weed free. Many gardeners leave parsnips in the ground until cold weather hits, believing the conversion of starch to sugar caused by the cold gives the root a sweeter flavor. The crop yield from a row 10 feet long will be about 10 pounds. Store in a cool place to prevent sprouting.

Parsnips are not attacked by many pests or diseases. Rust, sometimes seen on the leaves, does not hinder crop production unless the attack is severe. In such a case, a special spray for rust should be applied.

Many plants which grow in wild areas look like parsnips but are, in fact, poisonous. Eat only those you grow in your own garden or buy in the market.

PEA
Pisum sativum—garden pea
P. sativum var. *macrocarpum*—edible pod pea
Sun/light shade. 65-80 days to maturity.
In warm areas, sow September through April.
In cold areas, sow in spring as soon as ground
is workable; successive sowings.

For thousands of years peas were a popular household staple, probably due to the fact that they could be preserved so well in a dried form. Seeds of primitive peas have been found in mud where Swiss lake dwellers lived some 5000 years ago. Peas have also been found buried in caves in Hungary and on the site of ancient Troy.

The main centers of origin and development of the pea are northwest India through Afghanistan, Ethiopia and the Near East. Aryans from the East are said to have introduced the pea to the pre-Christian Greeks and Romans. The pea was grown originally for its dried seeds; they were much smaller and darker in color than our garden types. There was no mention of this familiar variety until after the Norman Conquest when, in the 12th century, "green peas for Lent" were mentioned in some church writings.

Before the end of the 16th century, botanists in Belgium, Germany and England described many kinds of peas—tall and dwarf, with white, yellow and green seed colors and smooth, wrinkled or pitted seeds. In the 17th century peas were a fashionable delicacy in Europe. The aristocrats ate peas after dinner, before retiring, to prevent indigestion. The English developed the finest varieties of pea; hence the common designation "English peas."

Peas vary in size and days to maturity but never in their need for cool growing temperatures. In cold areas they should be sown as soon as possible in the spring, with successive plantings every 10 to 15 days to maintain a continual supply. In warmer areas, where little frost is expected, sow as soon as day temperatures fall below an average of 75°F. Thus, in these warmer areas, sowing can begin in the early fall and continue into spring. The last sowing should be some 70 days before warmer days are expected. Make a little trench two to three inches deep, four to six inches wide and set the seeds out, spacing them about two to four inches apart. Cover the seeds with about one inch of soil. This will leave a

luna

108

shallow trench which allows for easy watering while the peas are growing. Overhead watering is not recommended as it could encourage mildew.

While all types of peas may be cultivated in this manner, it is best to plant the seeds of the climbing types about six inches apart in two distinct rows near the sides of the trench. A mesh netting may be hung to a line suspended between the rows. Twiggy sticks, no taller than four feet, may also be used. Some gardeners place a hoop of wire netting over the rows and allow the peas to ramble through. No matter which method you choose for these climbing types, all staking should be done when germination is visible and plants are just poking through the ground.

A 10-foot row of English peas will yield about three to four pounds a week. The edible pod pea, also called sugar pea or snow pea, will produce a little more than half that amount. As peas produce nitrogen in the soil, it is wise to follow them with a leaf crop which will be able to take advantage of this bonus.

Protect the young plants from snails and slugs. Apart from these pests, peas are, for the most part, disease free.

PEPPER
Capsicum frutescens
Sun. 110-140 days to maturity from seed,
   70-90 days from plants.
In warm areas, plant April/May.
In cold areas, plant May/June.

The intense interest lavished on the pepper plant by the early explorers in the New World and the records they kept describing the plant are unique in the history of American plants. Important food sources, such as the potato, were largely ignored. However, the explorers, to whom spices meant riches, thought these New World peppers a valuable find.

Columbus observed the natives of the West Indies growing and using fiery forms of *Capsicum*. He thought the plant to be another kind of the familiar black pepper and, even though not related, they share the common name "pepper." We know the Indians of South America used different types of peppers 2000 years ago. Fruits of the pepper plant are pictured in embroidery of an Indian garment found near the coast of Peru and believed to date to the first century. Wherever the early 16th century voyagers traveled in the American tropics—the West Indies, Central America, Mexico, Peru and Chile—they found forms of pepper. By the start of the 17th century, they had seen and recorded virtually every type known today.

Peppers were introduced into Spain in 1493. They were known in England by 1548 and in central Europe around 1585. In the 17th century the Portuguese took peppers to India and Southeast Asia. The growing temperatures being ideal in those parts of the world, the pepper flourished and became so common that their American origin was very often forgotten.

In the tropics the pepper is a perennial shrub. In our cooler climate they are treated as annuals. The plants vary greatly in shape and size. The pungent cherry pepper, which comes in red, yellow or purple, is round and usually one-half to one inch in diameter. The sweet or bell pepper is the most popular type for home gardening and is either long and tapering or blocky, with deep side grooves and a blunt tip. It is often picked while still green. It becomes red or a deep golden yellow if left to mature. Cayenne and chile peppers are slender and tapering. They grow to a length of one foot and are very hot. These are normally dried and ground into powders for use as condiments.

The simplest way to start peppers in the garden is to buy transplants at a nursery. However, you may start your own transplants from seed. Sow six to eight weeks before planting time in a three- to four-inch pot. Remove seedlings when they have grown to a height of two to three inches and set out, being certain that nighttime temperatures have stabilized at no lower than 55°F. Seed may also be planted outdoors by sowing in groups one inch deep and 18 inches apart in rows, allowing two feet between the rows. Thin the groups to one plant when they have reached a height of three inches. The ideal growing temperature is 80°F during the day and 65° at night. Keep well watered and mulch to hold the moisture, if necessary. In windy areas, staking is advised. As soon as the first flowers appear, feed the plant with a 5-10-10 fertilizer. The plants will produce fruit in 70 to 90 days. Make sure when harvesting the fruit that you always cut and never tear it.

Peppers make ideal container plants. In areas where the nighttime temperatures might fall below the safety level, the retained warmth of a wall near the container will protect the plant. Peppers are so colorful, you may want to fill many containers of different sizes to decorate your patio or deck.

Apart from the normal slugs and snails, peppers are not attacked by pests or diseases.

111

POTATO
Solanum tuberosum
Sun. 90 days to maturity.
In warm areas, plant February through May.
In cold areas, plant April/May.

The potato originated in the Peruvian Andes. Prehistoric tribes of that region carried the plant to other parts of South America but it was unknown in Central and North America until European explorers discovered and introduced it on their travels northward. Then these voyagers took the potato back home across the Atlantic and Sir Walter Raleigh planted potatoes in Ireland in the year 1585. The rest is history.

Preparation of the soil in which potatoes are to be grown should begin the fall preceding spring planting. Because the tubers (potatoes) are actually produced underground, the soil must be worked to as great a depth as possible. The soil should then be left in a rough state so that the winter weather can break it down still further. The soil can be of any type, but must have good drainage. Just before planting, a good layer of compost should be dug into the soil and an application of a complete fertilizer given. Potatoes like full sun. Plant as soon as possible in the spring, about 20 days before the last frost is due.

Propagate potatoes from "seed potatoes," which can be purchased at a nursery or from a mail-order house. You may also use potatoes from the market, but make sure they are the variety which will sprout. Frequently potatoes have been sprayed to prevent sprouting in storage. Cut a medium-sized tuber into about four pieces, making sure each section has one or two "eyes" from which the sprouts emerge. Place each section in a four-inch-deep, six-inch-wide trench, with a space of eight to 12 inches between plantings and two and a half to three feet between rows. Fill in the trench. As the sprouts emerge, keep all but the top four inches covered; use the soil from between the rows for this "earthing up." When the plants have been "earthed up" three or four times and the rows are eight to 10 inches above ground level, do not mound any more soil. The potatoes will mature in about 90 days. You should test a plant or two to see how the tubers are for size. Sometimes an extra week in the ground will make a tremendous difference in the size of the potato. New potatoes should be dug when the foliage begins to flower; mature potatoes when the vines

begin to die down. One plant grown to maturity will yield six to eight pounds of potatoes. Store until ready to use in a cool dark place.

Diseases such as scab, potato blight and wart disease can disfigure potatoes but do not make them unfit for consumption. Simply cut away the affected areas before cooking. If potatoes are grown from good seed stock and if good garden hygiene is employed, most diseases can be avoided.

RADISH
Raphanus sativus
Sun/light shade. 20-40 days to maturity,
   depending on variety.
In warm areas, sow September through April.
In cold areas, sow March/April.

The Latin name of this vegetable is a clue to its nature: translated, it means "easily reared." Radishes were a common food in Egypt long before the pyramids were built and the ancient Greeks made replicas of the radish in gold. In the Orient, where the radish is believed to have originated, ones weighing several pounds each are grown, a marked contrast to the small salad varieties popular in this country.

The salad radish is a quick-growing annual. It comes in various shapes, from round and cherry size to oblong and carrotlike, but these all have one thing in common—a very short maturity time. Because of this quick growth, radish seed can be mixed and sown with seeds of longer-maturing vegetables. The radish seed will germinate in five or six days and mark the rows so that cultivation can begin before the other seeds germinate. Allow the radish to mature and pull immediately.

Radish seed can be sown in the very early spring in cold areas as soon as frost has passed, and from September through April in warm areas. The seeds will grow in almost any type of soil but prefer a sandy loam with high organic content. A dressing of a 10-10-10 fertilizer a few days before sowing will see the crop through to maturity. To plant as a separate crop, sow the seeds in well cultivated soil about one-half inch deep. Thin the plants to two to three inches apart as soon as they are up. Make sure there is adequate moisture during the growing period and harvest when just ready or the flesh will become woody.

114

luna

The disease which most commonly attacks radish crops is mildew. Keeping the rows adequately thinned and maintaining good garden hygiene should keep trouble to a minimum. Most pests you discover, like slugs and snails, can be picked off and destroyed.

The large Oriental radish takes 60 days from seed to maturity. Seed should be sown in July and August and the plants thinned to eight to nine inches apart when up. Harvest promptly to avoid a woody texture.

RHUBARB
Rheum Rhaponticum
Sun/light shade. Two seasons to maturity.
In warm areas, plant January through March.
In cold areas, plant March/April.

Rhubarb is native to Siberia and Mongolia as well as parts of China and Tibet. The earliest records of rhubarb date from 2700 B.C. and were found in China. They describe the uses of the root for medicinal purposes. This rhubarb, however, was a different type from our common variety, which is a native of the eastern Mediterranean and has roots so potent that if consumed could cause violent digestive disturbances. The leaves and leaf blades of our rhubarb are also harmful enough to cause very serious illness, even death. The stalks, which we do eat, are perfectly harmless.

Rhubarb, of the garden type, was being cultivated in Italy in 1608. In the early 1700's it was becoming known in the rest of Europe and England, but it wasn't until the late 1700's that it was established as a food plant. It was, and still is, used primarily for making pies and tarts. Rhubarb was introduced into the United States in 1806, 200 years after it was first cultivated in Europe.

Rhubarb is rarely grown from seed because the results are so unpredictable. The best method of propagation is to buy two or three young plants from the nursery and set them out in the garden. Rhubarb can be grown in almost any ground but thrives especially well in a light, rich soil which contains ample moisture. It prefers full sun but can be grown in lightly shaded areas as well. It profits from heavy feedings of manure or compost and should be fertilized once a year as growth commences. Planting should be done in the early spring

as soon as the ground can be worked and the danger of frost is over. Plants should be spaced three feet apart. Rhubarb plants should not be harvested until the second year and then only in small amounts. A bed will remain productive longer if the plants are allowed to become well established before intensive harvesting begins. Stalks may be harvested until the plant sends up a flower spike, usually in late summer. At this time it is wise to stop harvesting and allow the plant to gather strength for the next growing season. Two or three plants will serve an average family's needs.

Every four years or so you may want to replace your rhubarb to encourage tender young growth. (Some gardeners prefer to leave rhubarb in place much longer—eight to 10 years.) Replacement is best done by root division. The root is lifted and chopped into pieces, making sure each piece contains one or more "eyes" or buds, like those of a potato. The new shoots will emerge from these eyes. Plant the root sections just under the soil about three feet apart, with the eyes facing up. If you wish to reap your rhubarb harvest earlier in the year, you may easily force the roots. Lift roots in the fall and leave them on the ground so they will be hit by frosts. In January, pack the roots into a large box and place it in a warm spot in the basement or garage. Keep moist with tepid water. The shoots will soon emerge and grow quickly. You may then plant the whole root or divide as described before.

Rhubarb may also be forced into earlier growth by covering the roots which you have planted in the ground. You may use any means of protection from a bucket to a cardboard box to a heavy layer of straw. The object is to keep the ground temperature warm, thereby forcing the shoots to develop early.

The most common problem in the propagation of rhubarb is crown rot. Since there is no effective control, you must dig up and discard any infected plants. Make sure not to put healthy crowns in the same area. Rust spots sometimes appear on the leaves of the plant but they do not weaken the rhubarb in any way.

RUTABAGA
Brassica Napobrassica
TURNIP
Brassica Rapa
Sun. Rutabaga, 85-90 days to maturity;
    turnip, 40-60 days.
Warm areas, sow September through April.
Cold areas, sow March/April, August/September.

The turnip is prehistoric, the rutabaga almost modern. Most varieties of turnip are white fleshed, while those of rutabaga are yellow fleshed. The leaves of the turnip are rough with stiff hairs covering them; those of the rutabaga are smooth like cabbage leaves.

The turnip originated in western Asia and in the eastern Mediterranean region and spread over most of Asia. In Europe the turnip has been used for food and as stock feed since the first century A.D. In the England of Henry VIII, turnip roots were boiled or baked, the tops cooked as greens and the young shoots used for salad. Jacques Cartier brought turnips to Canada in 1541. They were planted in Virginia by colonists in 1609 and in Massachusettes in 1620.

Rutabaga derives its name from the Swedish *rotabagge.* In England and Canada it is commonly called Swede or Swedish turnip. The story of the rutabaga is a very unusual one in the plant world. It seems at some point in history a rather rare kind of hybridization between a form of cabbage and one of turnip produced a new species, rutabaga. No one knows exactly when this occurred, but it was discovered in the late Middle Ages and described by the Swiss botanist, Casper Bauhin, in 1620. Rutabagas were grown in England's royal gardens in 1664. They were quite popular in France and southern Europe at this time as well.

Both vegetables are cool-weather crops. The turnip will produce in 40 to 60 days after the seed is sown. The rutabaga takes 85 to 90 days to produce a crop. Neither vegetable will survive if grown during a season when the daytime temperatures are 80°F or higher. In warm areas of the country, seeds should be sown in the spring, two months before 80° temperatures are expected. A fall crop may be planted if timed for harvesting before temperatures fall to 25° or below. Where little or no frost is expected, sowings may be made through winter.

luna

120

In cool areas of the country, sow seed in spring as soon as the ground can be worked. Two or three sowings may be made a few weeks apart for a prolonged harvest. Another crop or two may be started in late summer after day temperatures drop below 80°.

Before planting, work the ground well with a large quantity of humus. Save the most rock-free soil in the garden for turnips and rutabagas and any other root crops you may be planning. Stony or rocky soil can cause a root crop to be misshapen. After the soil has been worked, add fertilizer (six to eight ounces to every 10 feet of row) which is high in phosphate and low in nitrogen and potash. Rake the fertilizer into the soil.

Sow the seed thinly in half-inch deep drills, leaving 12 inches between the rows. After germination, when the seedlings are three to four inches high, thin the plants out to three inches apart. Leave about one-half inch more space between the rutabagas. As soon as the thinning is done, apply more fertilizer along the rows. Adequate moisture should be maintained at all times during the growing period. Keep the area well weeded. Turnips and rutabagas are relatively pest and disease free.

SORREL
Rumex Acetosa
Sun/light shade. 60 days to maturity.
Sow March/April.

Sorrel grows abundantly in meadows and forest glades. It is a slender plant, about two feet high, with fleshy leaves that have a delightful, slightly lemony taste. Sorrel has been used since ancient times as a salad green and, in France especially, has long been added to ragouts and soups. In England, around the time of Henry VIII, this plant enjoyed a great popularity. However, as other, more exotic leafy vegetables were introduced and cultivated, sorrel lost its favor.

Sorrel is a perennial. It thrives in deep, moist soil which has a high proportion of organic material. In warm areas it can be grown in partial shade but normally prefers sun. Once established, it may be left alone to provide a nutritious vegetable year after year.

It is best to start sorrel in the early spring so it is well established by the time winter

comes. Sow seed in drills one and a half inches deep, spacing the rows 18 inches apart. When the seedlings are three inches high, thin to 10 to 12 inches between plants. Make one application of a balanced fertilizer when the plants are six to eight inches high. This should be in the late spring. Follow with another feeding in midsummer. Once established, feed each year as soon as growth is visible in the spring. Harvest will be eight weeks after seed is sown or when new growth commences each spring. Cut leaves within one inch of the soil and they will grow again for a second cutting. Keep cutting and do not allow the plant to flower or the leaves will develop a bitter taste.

Of the two types of sorrel available, British and French, the latter is slightly more acid to the taste. Sorrel is free of pests and diseases with the exception of those persistent leaf eaters, slugs and snails.

SPINACH
Spinacia oleracea
Shade. 40-65 days to maturity, depending
    on variety.
In warm areas, sow August through April.
In cold areas, sow March/April and
    July/August.

Spinach is native to Iran and surrounding areas. Cultivation had spread to China, by way of Nepal, around 647 A.D. Ancient writings indicate the Moors, who had discovered spinach in the Middle East, brought it to Spain from North Africa in 1100. The prickly seeded spinach was known in 13th-century Germany and was commonly grown in European monastery gardens by the 14th century. Recipes for its preparation were contained in a cookbook used in the court kitchen of Richard II. Smooth-seeded spinach was first described in 1522. Spinach, like so many other vegetables common in Europe, arrived in America with the early settlers.

Warm weather will make spinach plants bolt (go to seed), which stops leaf production. Because of this tendency, it is fortunate that the time between sowing and harvesting is only six weeks. If the cool season is short, choose a variety that is less susceptible to bolting. In warm areas, where temperatures do not fall below 28°F, sow the seed every six weeks starting in late summer. In cool areas, sow the seed as soon as frosts have subsided in the spring.

124

Make two sowings, six weeks apart, using bolt-resistant varieties. Sow again in late summer. The final sowing should be six to eight weeks before hard frosts are due.

The ground should be well prepared before sowing, and because this is a cool weather vegetable, in a location that is shaded by trees or buildings. Sow seeds in half-inch deep drills in rows spaced one foot apart. When the seeds have germinated and the plants stand three to four inches high, thin them to three inches. As spinach is a leaf crop, nitrogen, in the form of 10-10-10 fertilizer, should be applied along the rows after the first thinning. A second thinning should be done when the plants are touching so that they then stand six inches apart. Leaves may be harvested when they reach a height of seven inches. When harvesting, remove the entire plant.

An adequate water supply must be provided at all times to insure abundant leaf production. Heavy soaking along the rows is advised. Mulching will also help to preserve moisture.

Two diseases which attack spinach are mildew and yellows, called this because it turns the leaves yellow. Fortunately there are varieties available which are resistant to these diseases. The usual slug and snail problems should be kept under control.

There are two types of spinach, smooth leaf and crinkled leaf. Both varieties provide good eating. It would be beneficial to try growing each type to see which you prefer, both for flavor and growing ease. A four-foot row of spinach will produce about one and a half pounds of leaves and thinnings.

SUMMER AND WINTER SQUASH
Cucurbita Pepo, C. Pepo var. *Melopepo,*
   C. maxima, C. moschata
Sun/light shade. 50-60 days to maturity for
   summer squash, 85-100 days for winter.
In warm areas, sow March.
In cold areas, sow May.

Squashes originated in the Americas. It wasn't, however, until they were transported to the European continent by early explorers that they became a culinary delicacy which was then returned to the Western World by the colonists. Both European and American gardeners still grow many varieties which are substantially the same as those grown by the pre-Colombians.

Summer squashes, which have become most popular in America, have long been favorites in Italy, as indicated by the names of the varieties developed there, cocozelle and zucchini. The fruits of the summer squash varieties must be harvested while they are young and the rind is not yet developed. It requires only four to six days after bloom for a fruit of most of these varieties to reach harvest stage. After two or three more days they are too old and tough to be desirable.

The flesh of the summer squashes is white or yellow, while that of the winter squash is orange; both types have plants which trail 12 feet or more in season. The bush types usually grow to four or five feet and are preferable for gardeners with limited space.

While all types of squash thrive best in full sun, the winter varieties will tolerate light or high shade. Seed of both winter and summer squash should be sown outdoors when the nighttime temperatures have reached a level of 50°F or warmer. Squash may be planted in rows five to six feet apart, or in mounds, which are preferred.

Prepare the ground for planting in this manner. Remove the soil from a selected area to form a hole six inches deep and two to three feet in diameter. Fill the hole with well-rotted compost or dung, digging it well into the bottom. Mix compost or dung with the soil you removed to dig the hole and fill it in again. Keep piling the soil until you have made a mound about six to eight inches high. The mounds should be about four feet apart to grow the bush types. Sow six seeds either in three clumps of two or in a circle, spacing the seeds four inches apart. When the seedlings are growing well, remove all but the strongest two in each mound. Remember to allow a good distance between plants. Water in well after these weaker plants have been removed and keep a good supply of water going to them all summer. Sufficient moisture is important during the growing season. After the plants have been established for about five weeks, give them a dressing of one-half soil, one-half compost. Liquid fertilizer will also benefit the plants. It should be applied once a month after a good watering. Normally, two vines will produce four pounds of fruit every two weeks and continue to so produce until the advent of the first frost.

If you wish to avoid sowing seed outdoors and are planning to set out young plants, do so when the night temperatures have reached an average of 50°F. Seed can be started indoors four weeks before young plants are to be set out. Seed should be sown, two to a pot, at a depth of one inch. Use seed compost with an addition of one-fourth part well-rotted manure or compost. Keep moist and remove the weaker seedling when three to four inches high. Plant out in the garden in mounds or rows. The first fruit should be ready for harvesting about seven to eight weeks after the seed is sown. Remove male blossoms so they cannot pollinate the already fruiting female flowers. (These blossoms may be eaten, raw or cooked.) As mentioned earlier, do not allow the fruit of the summer squash to stay on the vine too long. The winter type, however, should be allowed to ripen on the vine, so that the skin becomes hard. All types of squash should be cut rather than pulled from vine to avoid damaging the fruit and vine.

Keep a watch out for slugs on developing fruit. Mildew may occur if the weather is muggy. Removal of a few leaves will allow better air circulation and check the incidence of mildew without harming the plants.

TOMATO
Lycopersicon esculentum
Sun. 60-90 days to maturity from plants,
    110-150 from seed, depending on variety.
Plant after all danger of frost.

This familiar salad vegetable originated in the Andes. It was introduced into Europe in the 16th century and was regarded as a decorative plant. The first record of this plant being grown in the United States is on the Virginia farms of Thomas Jefferson in 1781. While tomatoes were eaten in New Orleans in 1812, they were not commonly grown for food in the northeast until some 25 years later. In fact, the myth that the fruit was poison was prevalent as recently as 50 years ago.

Tomatoes come in all colors, sizes and shapes. The color of the fruit can vary from the familiar red to yellow, with some varieties having a pink and others an orange color when ripe. The sizes range from small cherry types to large fruit weighing over one pound each. Shapes can be round, flat or pear.

There are two basic "forms" of tomato plant: the determinate, which will stop bearing when full grown and reaches a height of three feet or less, and the indeterminate, which will continue to bear as long as the plant grows. The latter is trained on a trellis or staked. Both types can be grown in containers, but the determinates are ideal for container growing as they form an attractive bushy plant. Varieties of different colors and shapes are available in both forms.

The time from setting out plants to the first harvest can vary from 60 to 90 days. If determinates are grown for early maturing, plan a second crop some 30 days after the first planting. They should then begin to bear as the first crop is finishing.

Tomatoes may be either started from seed or young plants can be purchased at a nursery. Sow seeds (seven to eight weeks before the last frost or in late December in frostless zones) in flats, making sure they are well spaced and lightly covered with one-fourth inch of soil. A soil mix of three parts loam or topsoil, two parts peat moss or leaf mold and one part sand is good. As the seedlings are susceptible to many diseases it is best to use a sterilized soil mix. Water in well and cover the flat with a pane of glass. A nighttime temperature of 75°F should be maintained, and as soon as the seeds germinate, remove the glass. Keep the flats moist at all times. When seedlings are two inches high, pot them up individually in four- to five-inch pots using the 7-3-2 soil mix described on page 34. Keep the plants in 65° to 70°F temperatures and provide maximum light so that the plants do not become leggy. As the time of transplanting nears, reduce the nighttime temperature so that the temperature outdoors will not adversely affect the plants.

If buying young plants at the nursery, select short sturdy ones. Even if they are a little leggy, do not worry. The plants can be put in the soil deeply and fresh roots will be produced along the stem that is buried. For this reason the plants should be planted with the first leaves resting on the soil. If the stems are very long, they can be laid in a trench as long as the shoot is upright. Place the plants two and a half to three feet apart. Water in well, and for the first few nights cover with plastic or paper to provide extra warmth. Cloches can be used to protect the plants when they are first set out, permitting planting two weeks earlier. Hence a longer season and more fruit result.

Tomatoes require well-worked soil with good drainage, plenty of compost or humus and sun. If planted against a wall, make sure there is enough space between the plants and wall for good air circulation. This will cut down the chance of mildew and other diseases. This space will also protect the plants from too much reflected heat which can burn the plant and the fruit. Once the plants are set out, it is necessary to provide a wooden stake of at least five feet in height (or some comparable means) to keep the indeterminate plants upright. If cloches are being used, the stakes are put in after the cloches are removed.

When the plants are first set out they can be interplanted with lettuce or a sowing of radish. Both of these plants will have been harvested before the tomato plants start to crowd them out.

At all times during the growing season, the tomato should be supplied with sufficient moisture. A dry spell can cause the fruit to crack and interrupt the continued growth which is necessary for a good crop. A 5-10-10 fertilizer should be used for tomatoes. The effect of too much nitrogen is too much foliage and reduced fruit production. An initial application at planting time or just prior will serve the plants until the first fruit is set. Each month after that a dressing should be given.

The fruit should always be kept off the soil. Bush-type tomatoes can be trained in a wire-netting cage or by the use of small stakes with string ties. Support for developing fruit may be needed if the plants are in containers, as the weight of the fruit is sometimes sufficient to break the stems without such support.

I find the following the best way to train indeterminate plants for the maximum production of fruit per square foot of soil. On each plant, allow the first two side shoots to develop and remove all others. (In areas with a long growing season, 150 to 180 days, allow three side shoots.) Tie the shoots to the stake or support securely but not too tightly. Stop the first side shoot after the second truss of flowers is produced. This is done by removing the growing shoot above the flowers. The second and third shoots are allowed to produce only one truss of flowers before being pinched back.

As the main stem develops, keep it supported to the stake. When the first fruit is set on the lower trusses, remove about half of the leaves below the fruit. At the same time remove some of the leaves that are shading the fruit so the air can circulate around the fruit, but leave enough foliage to protect the tomatoes from too much direct sun. After the first truss of fruit is harvested, remove the leaves below the truss and thin above the second truss. Carry on in this manner until, at the end of the season, the lower part of the plant is bare of leaves. As the season ends, about two weeks before the first frost is due, remove any leaves that are shading the fruit to help the sun ripen them.

This method of growing reduces the bulkiness of the plants and allows closer planting to be done—two and a half feet rather than the usual three. The result is higher yield per foot of row planted.

There are variations on the row method of planting which can be tried. Either a trellis or a tall stake with strings or wires at the top, maypole fashion, can be used for each plant. The pruning method is the same as described above for either case. In areas with a very long growing season the plants can be removed from the support, stems laid down on the ground, buried and the tops trained up again. Roots will form along the stem.

The addition of a mulch during the growing season will also promote new roots. Grass clippings or well-rotted compost can be used, as well as peat moss, leaf mold or other

luna

substances which will allow new roots to penetrate. Bark chips, for instance, are not suitable.

During the growing season spray with a fine spray of cold water early in the morning before the sun is on the plants or in the evening when the sun is set. (This latter should not be done if the nights are below 55°F, as the plants will be "chilled.") The spraying will accomplish two things: First, it will help set the fruit by making the pollen move, and secondly it will discourage white fly, one of the most common pests. A hormone spray can also be used to increase the set of fruit, or you can hand-pollinate by moving the pollen from blossom to blossom with a clean cloth or sable brush.

Aphids can be a nuisance. Spray should be used only if it has been cleared for use on vegetable crops. Read the label carefully and follow the directions, especially with regard to the number of days the spray can be used prior to harvest.

The tomato is susceptible to a good number of diseases. Varieties are now available that are resistant to verticillium and fusarium wilt and to nematode attack. If you have grown tomatoes for years and the plants have consistently suffered from wilt and underproduction, try the wilt-free varieties. If the ground has not been used for tomatoes, grow the non-resistant varieties because they produce more flavorful fruit.

BASIL
Ocimum Basilicum
Sun. 40 days to maturity.
Sow March/April.

Superstitions of ancient civilizations bred fantastic legends. One of the strangest is about the sweet basil, a lovely scented herb used extensively throughout southern Europe in cooking. It was thought that if this plant were handled gently it yielded a pleasant smell, but if wrung or bruised would breed scorpions! It was also thought that a sprig of basil left under a pot would become a scorpion. The superstition went so far as to suggest that smelling the plant might bring a scorpion into the brain itself.

In India, however, the plant was sacred and kept in every Hindu house as a protecting

133

spirit. Good Hindus went to their final rest with a sprig of basil on their breast as a passport to Paradise.

Seed should be sown annually in the spring in a sunny location as soon as frost danger has passed. Sow the seed thinly in shallow drills. When the first growth appears, thin the plants to eight inches apart. Fresh basil leaves may be picked throughout the growing season. If they are to be dried and stored, harvest the leaves immediately after the plant has stopped blooming.

When winter comes, cut the plants back, pot them up, bring them into the house and set the pots on a sunny windowsill. This will permit the plants to yield a second smaller crop during the time of the year when the cold weather prevents their thriving outside.

CHIVE
Allium Schoenoprasum
Sun/light shade. 80 days to maturity from
    seed, 30 days from plants.
Plant March/April.

The chive is the smallest, though one of the finest flavored, of the onion tribe. It belongs to the same group of plants which includes garlic, leek and shallot. Chives are found growing in a wild state in almost all parts of the world. In Corsica and Greece, the south of Sweden, in Siberia as far as Kamschatka and in North America. Oddly enough, though the plant is said to be a native of Britain, it is rarely seen growing there in an uncultivated state. The chive was probably known to ancient man. In 812 A.D. Emperor Charlemagne included chives on a list of plants to be grown in the royal garden. Chives are mentioned in a 15th-century British cookbook.

The chive contains, in common with all members of the onion family, a pungent volatile oil, which is rich in sulphur and causes the familiar taste and smell. The chive is a great addition to salad, is excellent in egg dishes and can be used in soups and casseroles, sprinkled on mashed potatoes and even eaten plain.

A perennial, chive bulbs grow very close together in dense tufts or clusters. The slender leaves appear in early spring and are long and hollow, tapering to a point. The flowering

134

135

stem is usually nipped off, as the plants are grown most often for the sake of the leaves. Were you to allow the plant to flower, you would see at the tip of the flowering stem a globular head of purple flowers. The blossoms appear in June and July and in cold, moist situations will mature their seeds. When dried, these flowers become a lovely shade of rose.

Though chives can be grown from seed, it is best to buy small clumps of this very hardy bulb and plant them in a row eight inches apart. The clumps will soon form one continuous row. They may be used effectively to edge a flower or vegetable bed. Chives demand little room and will multiply in any garden soil of moderate condition with adequate moisture. At the end of summer the plants may be lifted, placed in a pot and kept on a kitchen windowsill. By doing this, you will be able to enjoy this fine herb during the winter months.

The bulbs which are left in the ground will go dormant. They will come up again in the spring and continue, in this manner, to produce for many years. The only disease which is likely to attack the plants is rust. Should this occur, throw the plant away and start again. With this one exception, chives are virtually foolproof!

CORIANDER
Coriandrum sativum
Sun/light shade. 30 days to maturity.
In warm areas, sow January/February.
In cold areas, sow March/April.

Coriander, also known as cilantro and Chinese parsley, is a very attractive herb. It has a round stalk, about two feet in height, laden with branches. The leaves resemble flat-leaf parsley but become jagged as they mature. The flowers are white and grow in round tassels like dill. The seeds are tiny round balls and have a very disagreeable scent which dissipates on drying. They then become nicely fragrant. The longer the seeds are kept, the more pleasant their aroma grows.

Coriander was originally introduced to the Western World from the Orient, and was one of the herbs brought to Britain by the Romans. As an aromatic stimulant and spice, it has been cultivated and utilized from very ancient times. It is used in all parts of the East as

137

a condiment and forms an ingredient in curry powder. The Egyptians use the leaves in soup. The Africans use it in much of their cooking. The natives of Peru are so fond of the taste and smell of this herb that it is a part of almost all their dishes. It has been used in the medicine world since the days of Hippocrates.

Pliny, the great Roman historian and naturalist, derived the name *Coriandrum* from *koros* (an insect), in reference to the fetid smell of the leaves. Pliny wrote that the best coriander came from Egypt and during their years in bondage in that land, the Israelites, too, learned of its properties. In northern Europe, the seeds are sometimes mixed in bread but the chief use of coriander seed in that part of the world is for flavoring certain alcoholic beverages. In England, it is grown in Essex for use in the distilling of gin.

Coriander is an annual and is so easy to grow, the seeds germinating quite readily, that many people think it is a perennial. Seed sown in spring, after the danger of frost has passed, will reach a height of one to one and a half feet by the end of summer. Coriander will grow in full sun or high light shade in almost any well-drained soil and does well when planted in the company of dill and chervil. Sprigs may be clipped like parsley during the summer months. When the growing season has ended, the plants should be harvested and the seeds thrashed out, dried and stored.

DILL
Anethum graveolens
Sun. 40-50 days to maturity.
Sow in spring as soon as ground is workable.

Dill is a hardy annual native to the Mediterranean region and southern Russia. It has been used from earliest times as a drug. The name itself, derived from the Norse "dilla," means to lull. It has extraordinary effects as a carminative medicine and is often used in treating children suffering from severe stomach pains. In the Middle Ages it was kept around by sorcerers, wizards and magicians for use in casting spells and as an ingredient in charms related to witchcraft.

Today the leaves of the dill plant are used fresh and dried in cooking. They have a very light clean taste and are delicious in fish or egg dishes. The seeds are used in pickling.

Seed is sown in early spring, as soon as the ground can be worked. Sow thinly, leaving a space of 10 inches between the rows. When the first growth appears, thin the plants to eight inches apart. The leaves should be picked as soon as the flowers begin to open. Tie in bunches and hang upside-down in a dry place. When the leaves and flower heads have dried, remove them from the stalks and store leaves and seeds separately.

GARLIC
Allium sativum
Sun. 120 days to maturity from seed, 90 days
    from bulbs.
In warm areas, sow January, plant February/
    March, October-December.
In cold areas, sow March/April, plant May.

Because the garlic plant has been cultivated from ancient times, it is difficult to write with any true authority about its early origins. We do know it was indigenous to the southwestern region of Siberia. From there it was transported by wandering tribes and traders in many directions, including the Mediterranean region of Africa and Europe where it became naturalized. It is also widely cultivated in the Latin countries.

Garlic has been believed for centuries to ward off evil spirits, and as a protection from vampires. It was also used as a preventative against infectious diseases, fevers, plague and even leprosy. An old journal relates that early in the 19th century during an outbreak of an infectious fever in a poor quarter of London, the French priests, who constantly used garlic in all their dishes, visited the worst cases with impunity. English clergymen, however, caught the infection and fell victims to the disease.

Garlic is a hardy plant, easy to grow and reputed to be a "pest preventer" in the garden. Sandy soil with a generous amount of organic material present will produce the best crops. While garlic can be grown from seed, it is advisable to start from bulbs. Plant in early spring. Break the bulbs up into cloves and plant, not too deeply, base end down six inches apart. When the plants begin to show some green foliage, dress with a 10-10-10 fertilizer. This should be repeated two or three times at three-week intervals. Keep the plants well

watered during the growing period. When summer comes to an end, even though the temperature might still be quite hot, stop watering. Bend the tops over the bulbs to expose them to the sun. This procedure hastens the ripening process. Harvest the bulbs in the fall when the leaves have died, twine the tops together to form a pigtail and hang in an airy place to dry. Select small cloves for planting the following year.

In mild-winter areas, garlic can be planted from October through December for an early summer harvest.

MARJORAM
Majorana hortensis
Sun. 30-40 days to maturity.
Sow in March/April.

Native to North Africa, sweet marjoram is considered sacred to Siva and Vishnu in the Hindu religion. Like its cousin oregano, it was used in medicines in ancient times. It is a fine plant for containers and does especially well in the sunnier areas of rock gardens. While it is a perennial and can easily be started from cuttings or by division, it is so easy to raise from seed that I would recommend a fresh sowing each spring. Marjoram is not fussy as to soil, but does like full sun and not too much moisture during the summer months.

MINT
Mentha species
Light shade. 30 days to maturity from root
 divisions.
Plant March/April.

There are three chief species of mint in cultivation: spearmint *(Mentha viridis)*, peppermint *(M. piperita)* and pennyroyal *(M. Puleglium)*. All three yield a fragrant oil by distillation. The plant is a native of the Mediterranean region and has been so universally esteemed that it is to be found growing in nearly all civilized parts of the world.

The ancients used mint to scent their bath water and as a restorative, much in the way smelling salts are used today. There were at least 40 distinct maladies for which mint was "singularly good." Since the 14th century, mint has been used for whitening teeth and its distilled oil is still used to flavor toothpaste, candy, chewing gum and perfumed soap. Many people depend on mint tea as a calmative for upset stomach.

Mint will grow and produce foliage in almost any soil, but thrives best in a light, moist, organically rich one. It is possible to grow mint from seed, but the results are so often variable that this method of propagation is rarely used. The best method is to plant cuttings, using the young growth from mature plants. Mint may also be propagated by root division. Planting should be done in early spring in a partially shaded location for best results. Plant three to four feet apart, leaving a space of three feet between the rows. Once the plants are established, the roots become invasive and can intrude on other crops. Therefore, it is best to keep mint separated from your other plants. If space is limited, you can successfully grow mint in containers. Cut back each spring to promote new, vigorous growth. Replace plants every three years.

OREGANO
Origanum vulgare
Sun. 30-40 days to maturity from seed.
In warm areas, sow March.
In cold areas, sow April.
Plant divisions March/April.

In the time of Hippocrates, this herb was used to impart a pleasant smell to ointments. Oregano is a hardy perennial that grows well in containers. It is easily grown from seed or can be divided in the fall or early spring. A sunny location and well-drained soil will produce a full, thriving plant. While a perennial, it is best to replace plants after three or four seasons. If you wish the maximum production of leaves, cut the plants back during the growing season to encourage more foliage and inhibit flowering. Oregano is found growing wild in much of Europe.

PARSLEY
Petroselinium crispum
Sun/shade. 70-80 days to maturity.
Sow March/April.

Although the ancient Greeks held parsley in great esteem, they never ate it. They crowned their victors with it, they adorned their tombs with it, they even fed it to their strongest chariot horses. It was much too valuable a plant to waste at the table. Today, however, parsley is one of our most common cooking ingredients, and the stems are said to be an effective aphrodisiac, if eaten in great enough quantities. There are several different types of parsley—plain leaf, curled leaf and fern leaf, to mention a few. It is a plant which is extremely rich in both vitamins A and C.

Parsley is an easy plant to grow. The seeds, however, take a long time to germinate. Soaking the seeds in water for 24 hours prior to planting will help speed the germination. Plant seeds by broadcasting in a square and, when germination takes place, thin them to four inches apart. Seed may also be planted in rows and thinned to four inches. Harvest the sprigs throughout the growing season and as the season comes to an end, dry the leaves for winter use.

Parsley is a biennial but is best treated as an annual. In its second year it will produce little foliage because its strength is devoted to seed production.

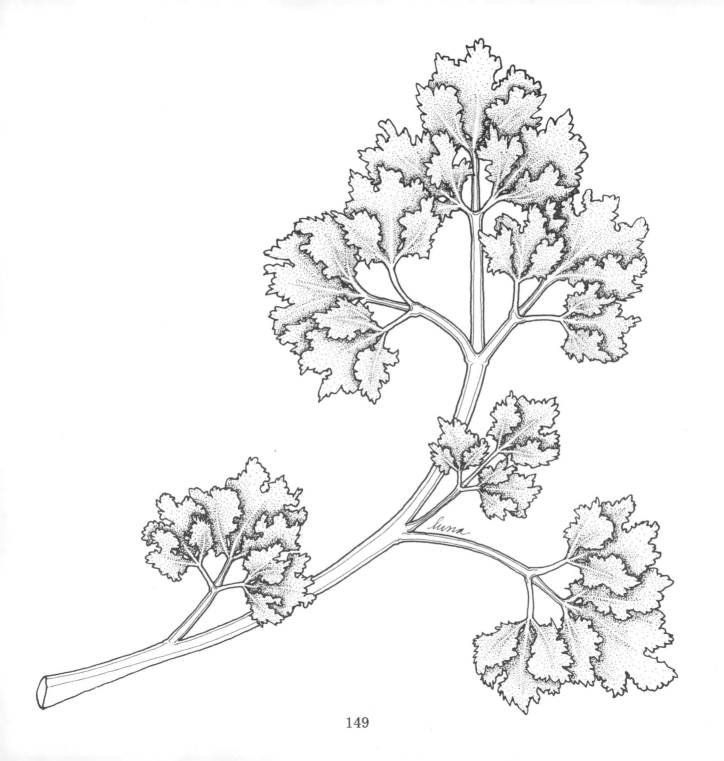

149

ROSEMARY
Rosmarinus officinalis
Sun. 40 days to maturity from cuttings.
Plant March/April.

Ancient peoples thought rosemary had powers to strengthen the memory. On this account it became the symbol of lovers. At weddings it was entwined in the wreath worn by the bride. Anne of Cleves wore such a wreath at her marriage to Henry VIII. Because of its association with memory, it was also used at funerals and was very often planted on graves. Sir Thomas More wrote: "As for Rosmarine, I lett it runne all over my garden walls, not onlie because my bees love it, but because it is the herb sacred to remembrance, and, therefore to friendship. . . ."

In early times it was also believed that "where rosemary flourished, the woman ruled." So touchy were many husbands on this point that they purposely injured a healthy plant in order to destroy any evidence of their lack of authority. In both Spain and Italy it is regarded as a safeguard from the evils of witchcraft. The Spaniards revere it as one of the bushes that gave shelter to the Virgin Mary in the flight to Egypt.

The shrub is a native to the Mediterranean region. It is a hardy evergreen with extremely slender leaves. Small blue flowers are produced along the axils of the leaves. The best method of propagation is to plant from cuttings. Rosemary does well in even a rather poor soil. This condition helps produce a greater amount of oil in the plant and, hence, a richer fragrance in the leaves. Plant in a sunny spot 18 inches apart, leaving a space of three feet between the rows. Rosemary can take a certain amount of winter cold but will not survive temperatures below 10°F. To produce maximum foliage, keep plants pinched back.

As it spreads rapidly, rosemary makes an excellent hedge. Plants should be replaced every few years. Use the sprigs fresh, or dry and store.

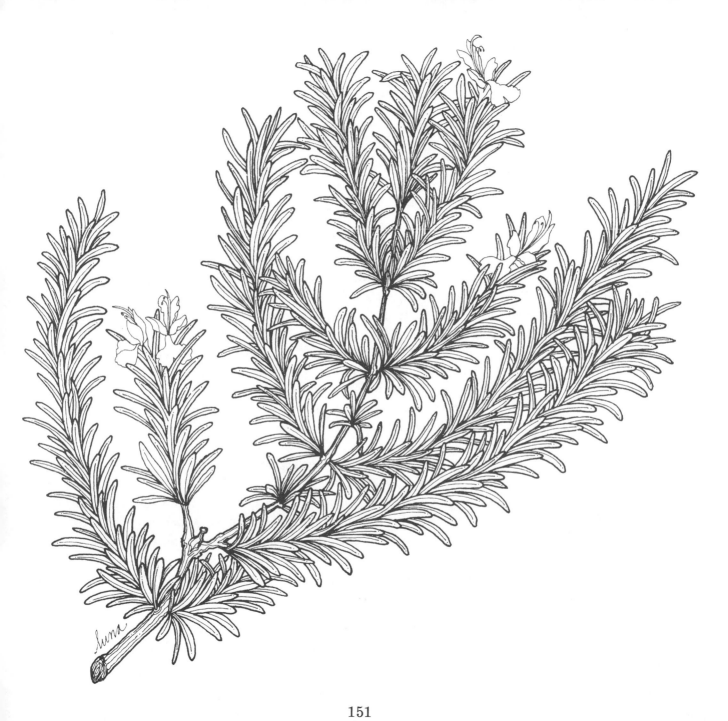

SAGE
Salvia officinalis
Sun. 50 days to maturity from cuttings.
Plant June.

Among the ancient tribes and throughout the Middle Ages, sage was held in the highest regard as a curative. There is a Latin phrase which translated means, "Why should a man die whilst sage grows in his garden." An old French poem reads, "Sage helps the nerves and by its powerful might/Palsy is cured and fever put to flight."

The Chinese were said to prefer sage tea to their own natural product. Throughout Europe, sage has always been thought of as beneficial to good health. It was mixed with vinegar and honey to soothe sore throat, heated with vinegar to make compresses for sprains, and was an aid in the treatment of liver diseases and to stop the flow of blood. Sage and vinegar tea was a popular beverage during times of plague.

The sage plant is an evergreen undershrub. Its natural habitat is the northern shores of the Mediterranean and it is found growing wild from Spain along the coast, up to and including part of the eastern side of the Adriatic coastline.

Sage can be grown from seed, but it is most frequently raised from cuttings, which root easily. These cuttings should be made in early summer before the wood becomes too hard. Plant the cuttings in a sunny location about 18 inches apart in a soil that is not too fertile. If grown in rich soil, the plants will become succulent and thereby much more susceptible to being killed by frost. The ground should be kept well weeded. Sage is remarkably pest and disease free.

As soon as the leaves and stems are of useable size they may be picked. They can be used fresh, or dried and then crushed.

153

TARRAGON
Artemisia Dracunculus
Sun. 30-40 days to maturity from root
    divisions.
Plant March/April.

Tarragon is a native of Siberia but has long been cultivated in France. Its name is a corruption of the French *esdragon* which means "little dragon." It is unusual that the name for this herb has the same general meaning in many diverse parts of the world.

The plant thrives in a warm dry location in a wide range of soils. If grown in cold areas, tarragon needs winter protection. The plants seldom produce fertile seed and, therefore, should be purchased and subsequently propagated by root division. The roots should be divided in March or April and planted 12 inches apart. The leaves may be picked in early summer and used fresh or they can be dried and stored in a well-ventilated place.

To keep the supply healthy, it will be necessary to lift and start new plants every three or four years; old plants will simply stop producing.

THYME
Thymus vulgaris
Sun. 30 days to maturity from root divisions.
Plant March/April.

The name thyme was first given to the plant by the Greeks as a derivative of a word which meant "to fumigate," either because they used it as incense for its balsamic odor or because it was looked upon as descriptive for all sweet smelling herbs. The plant was held, in medieval days, to be a great source of invigoration, its qualities inspiring courage. The ladies of this period embroidered their knightly lover's scarves with the figure of a bee hovering over a sprig of thyme. Today, thyme is used as a culinary herb, a medicine, and commercially as the source of the volatile oil thymol, which is used as a deodorant and anesthetic. Thyme probably has more practical uses than any other herb, besides its ornamental value in the garden.

This tough little plant is a hardy perennial. It can be raised from seed, but it is much easier to buy a small plant and divide the roots for planting. Planting should be done in the spring. Be sure to choose a location in which the plant will be exposed to full sun and plant 12 inches apart. Thyme prefers a rocky or gravelly soil. It is, however, a most accommodating plant, and, with the addition of a little sand to heavy soils, will grow just about anywhere.

Prune back in the spring to promote heavy growth. This will protect the roots from the ravages of freezing and thawing and freezing which can do damage to the plant. Thyme should be replaced every three or four years. This can be done by lifting the plants, selecting out the youngest roots and replanting them. The plant, which grows to a height of 10 or 15 inches, is so pretty it merits a place in an ornamental border. Harvest as required for daily use. If the leaves are to be dried, harvest just after the plant has come into full bloom. Dry the clippings and store in an airtight container.

Container Gardening

Early in his history the farmer learned which was the most propitious time to plant each crop and when the harvesting of that crop should begin in order to derive the greatest possible benefit from sun and rain. He was, however, left with the inevitability of winter and the resultant barren fields. Eventually, a method was devised whereby crops could flourish the year round. The farmer realized that by planting in containers which, when the cold weather commenced, could be moved to a more sheltered area or into the house itself, he perpetuated the growing season and provided his household with a food supply during the long winter.

Today, while container planting is still a valid method of protecting crops from winter frosts, it is also employed as a system whereby available space can be utilized to create a garden where only a deck, patio or balcony exists. In fact, because of increased interest in home gardening and the great numbers of people now living in apartments and townhouses, container gardening is enjoying a tremendous popularity. It affords those persons who could not previously grow crops because of a lack of land the opportunity to enjoy the peace, relaxation and sense of accomplishment embodied in the practice of gardening.

When planted directly in the ground, crops must absorb whatever sun, shade and moisture their positions allow. They are vulnerable to heavy rains and damaging winds. A crop grown in a container can be moved around to take advantage of the greatest sun or shade exposure, whichever it may require, and can also be sheltered from harsh weather. In addition to protection, planting a crop in containers enables the gardener who has adequate outdoor space to extend his growing season. He can start seeds indoors when, because of frost, planting them in the ground would be impossible. When the frost danger is passed and his plants have been established, he can set them out into the garden to mature.

The size and shape of the containers which you select vary, of course, with their ultimate function. Any vessel, from a tiny earthenware pot for chives to a large redwood planter for salad crops of cabbage, lettuce and tomatoes, may be classified as a potential container.

When selecting containers there are a few points to keep in mind. The soil in containers will dry out more quickly than that which is out in the garden. Daily doses of full sun may be too much for some crops and containers may need to be moved periodically. Because of the additional weight of the soil and moisture, moving a very large container from place to place may prove to be a back-breaking chore you had not forseen when admiring it empty at the nursery or garden center. Therefore, if you wish to plant a large crop in one container make certain it is one which will thrive in a permanent position.

There are several types of lightweight containers available for purchase. These are ideal for the gardener who must climb stairs or walk a distance with plants while doing gardening chores. Western Pulp Pots are made from waste paper mixed with a mulsified asphalt which does not injure plants. The pots will last for two years provided the bases are not left to stand in water. They are light brown in color and come in a variety of sizes.

One of these pots which is 12 inches in diameter, 11 inches deep and weighs one pound is ideal for growing a wide range of vegetables. A pot which is 18 inches in diameter, 16 inches deep and weighs just over three pounds would be perfect for any root crop. As these containers are made from recycled products and are very light, their use is to be encouraged.

Wooden containers can be built to suit specific needs. For example, a triangular-shaped planter can be constructed to fit into the corner of a deck, or a long narrow redwood planter can edge a walkway. In order to retard rot and invasion by pests, wooden containers should be treated with a protective coating, such as Cuprinol, which is permeable and non-toxic to plants. It is better to leave the natural wood rather than to paint the outside of the container.

Clay pots are preferable to ceramic because they are more porous. However, ceramic pots are so attractive you may wish to use some for their decorative value. Make certain the soil you use in such pots is very light and airy and never let it become firmly packed down. If you take these precautions, you should have no problem growing crops in ceramic containers.

Of course, these are the most obvious containers. You are limited only by your imagination—bushel baskets, half wine barrels, dishpans, washtubs. Be sure to allow for drainage by drilling holes in the bottom of the planter or your vegetables may become

waterlogged. As with ceramic pots, make sure the soil you are using is very light and airy if the container is of plastic or some other non-porous material.

After each harvesting the remaining soil should be augmented and mixed with the residual. Soil should be dumped once a year and the container should be filled with a fresh mix. There are several types of soil mixes available for container gardening. Made up of lightweight materials with slow release fertilizers, these mixes adapt readily to the cultivation of a wide range of plants. If you prefer to make up your own lightweight mixture, try the following:

> Seven parts soil (use planting mix or potting soil which
>   is sold commercially).
> Three parts peat moss or fir bark (not redwood bark as it is acid).
> Two parts builders' sand or perlite, sponge rock or similar product.
> To this add a slow release fertilizer in a formula of
>   13-6-6 or 8-4-4.

In any container, make sure that the drainage is good. If the container is flat then raise the bottom a little so that the water can escape. If you are diligent in this point you will find that successful cultivation can be achieved in any type of container be it clay, ceramic, wood or paper.

Many of the vegetables which follow have varieties available that have been specifically developed for container gardening. Most seed catalogs and nurseries highlight these varieties for the customer.

BEANS

Bush beans will start to yield a crop in 45 days. Do not try to sow seeds in containers but, rather, purchase young plants at the nursery. Plant three to an 18-inch pot; at least four pots will be required if you wish a good supply of beans. You can interplant the beans with radishes, which will mature in 20 days if they are sown in the spring. They will be ready to harvest before the beans become big enough to shield them from needed sun.

Pole beans should be grown only in large containers or in a long box which will accommodate the trellis framework of strings necessary for growing this type of bean. The containers can be placed against a wall or fence. If large containers are available and feasible in your growing area, use a tripod of sticks six feet in height upon which the beans may climb. Use two containers with a minimum of nine plants in each. Once these attractive plants have been started, a crop of lettuce may be grown in the center of each

163

tripod. The beans will shield the lettuce from too much sun. As both crops require ample amounts of water, they combine very successfully. Remember to keep the beans picked or they will stop producing.

BEETS
Sow seeds directly into containers. They will mature in about 55 to 65 days. Thin out plants when they start to crowd too much in the pot. The greens and small beets from these thinnings can be used in salads.

CARROTS
Since carrots, which mature in 60 to 80 days, can be harvested before the severe frosts arrive, they make an ideal crop to precede or follow one of the slower growing ones. There are many varieties of carrots which adapt well to container growing. The shorter types are, of course, better suited to pots and planters. Sow seed in shallow drills and thin out after the plants are started. These thinnings may be used in salads. In an area where summer is short, follow the carrot crop with bush beans, which take 45 to 70 days to mature, or with lettuce or radishes.

CAULIFLOWER
Sow seeds indoors and set out after the heat of summer is past, allowing 70 days before the first hard frost. In order to protect the developing flowers during mild frosts, break the leaves over the flower heads while they are maturing. Cauliflower can also be grown in the first part of the season (spring) if the plants are started indoors and set out in containers after all danger of frost is past. In this case, allow 70 days from planting to the time when warm nights are expected. These are large plants, so allow a good-sized deep container with good loam and drainage.

CHARD
Chard is a crop which is truly decorative as well as being nourishing. Plant four to six young plants in a large container. Keep picking off the outside leaves as they are needed. More will be produced and an ample supply for the family's consumption may be realized out of three containers. Try growing both the red-and-white-veined types. They are as beautiful as any flower on a deck or patio. To add extra color, plant a few trailing lobelia around the outside of the container. In an area where the frosts come early in the year, chard may occupy the

container for the whole season. If, however, you start it early it might be finished some time before the first frosts. If this is the case, follow the chard with a short-period vegetable such as radishes (20 days) or lettuce (45 days).

CUCUMBER

This is one of the vegetables which may be grown in a hanging container in a sunny location. It requires watering every day, so make sure you locate it in a place where the watering may be done with relative ease. If you wish, cucumbers may also be grown on a trellis in a large container. If your space is limited, however, and you do not wish to hang the plant, it would be wiser to choose the bush type which does not trail.

Remember to keep the fruit picked and to remove the male flowers (see page 92). Cucumbers like rich soil and profit from heavy feedings of liquid fertilizer once the plants have started active growth. They are best grown alone and will need high humidity and protection from cold.

EGGPLANT

Easily adapted to container growing, eggplants require a good deal of sun and are best planted two or three to a 12-inch pot. In cooler regions, place the container in the sunniest spot where any reflected heat from a wall can increase the temperature. If you live in an area where the summer is short, select the varieties which mature quickly. Do not combine eggplant with other vegetables in the container. When harvesting cut, do not pull, the fruit from the plant.

KOHLRABI

This is one of the few root-like vegetables which can be successfully grown in containers. Set out young plants as soon as possible after frost danger is past. Pick a cool location, as excessive heat will make plants bolt. Plant two or three young plants about five inches apart in a large container, or sow seeds directly and then thin to five inches apart. Keep them well watered. Make sure they are harvested while still growing. Many gardeners mistakenly allow the kohlrabi to mature beyond a three-inch diameter and the root becomes tough and stringy. Kohlrabi can stand small amounts of frost in the fall. Therefore, they may be grown for a fall crop as well, started after the hottest part of the summer is over.

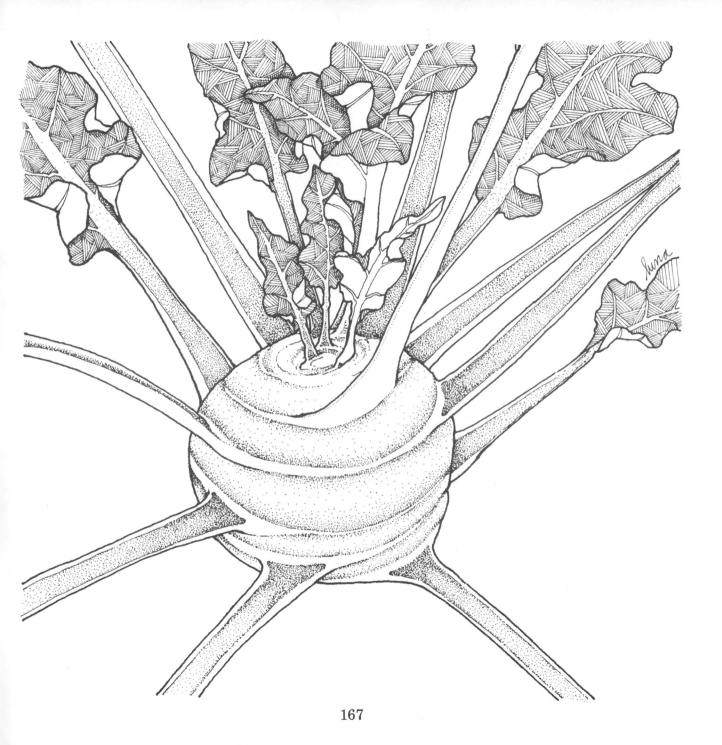

LETTUCE

Any variety of lettuce may be grown in containers. The container itself may be shallow, as lettuce does not require a great depth of soil in which to grow, but it should be good size. Set out the young plants as early in the spring as is possible. After harvesting, you may follow with a long summer crop such as the short varieties of carrots and then radishes. If you grow the lettuce in a fairly deep container, you may follow up with a crop of tomatoes and then cabbage. Lettuce must be harvested while still young. If you decide to replant lettuce in a container which has already produced a crop that year, make sure a good supply of well-rotted compost or steer manure is incorporated into the soil mix.

ONIONS

Because it s leaves turn yellow and can get to look messy, the large bulb onion is not the most attractive plant for container growing. As container plants are usually on view, green onions would be a wiser, more attractive choice. Green onions are planted very close together and a good supply can be had from one or two medium-sized containers. In container gardening it is best to start with onion sets of the bunching variety. Evergreen Bunching or any of the others listed in seed catalogues as "bunching" varieties will give good results. Do not plant the sets too deeply in the soil. If growing bulb onions, at least half the bulb should be exposed to the sun as this aids the ripening process. Remember to apply fertilizer at regular intervals until such time as the bulb is a good size and the tops have started to turn brown.

PEAS

Peas suitable for container growing come in two varieties: those which may be trained to grow up a trellis of chicken wire (this type may also be used in hanging containers) or those short types which bush. Peas do not thrive in the high temperatures of summer, so in cold areas, sow seed as soon as possible in the spring (March through May). In warmer areas seeds should be sown in January and February and again in September. Cowpeas or Southern table peas prefer the heat and are killed by the slightest frost. Sow these after all frost

danger is passed and make successive sowings. Always remove pods as they mature, harvesting in the cool of the morning while they are still plump. Plan on three plants of the bush type to a large container or five to six plants for a trellis arrangement, which can extend over the sides of the container. Feed when the plants are established and never allow them to become dry. Follow peas with lettuce, chard, sorrel or carrots. The yield of each plant is not great, so several containers of peas should be cultivated.

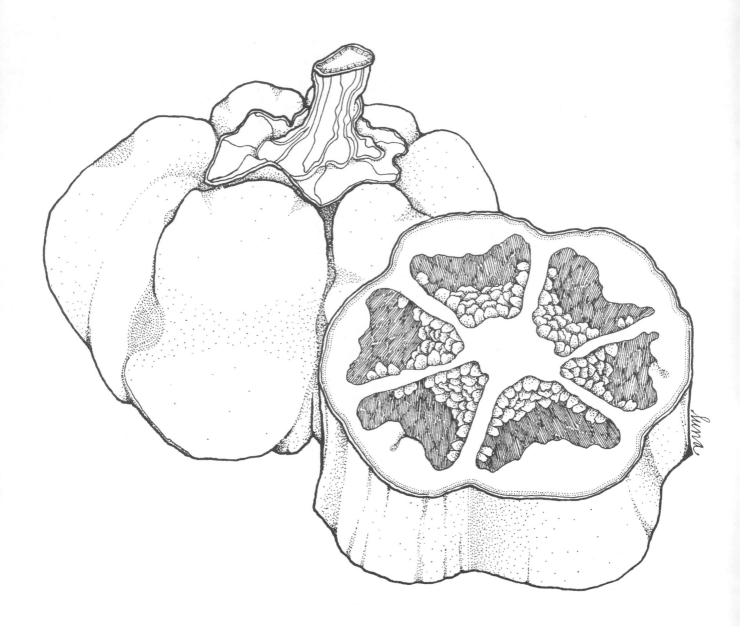

PEPPERS

Set the pepper plants out after the frost danger is over. They prefer day temperatures of 75°F with night temperatures of 65°F. The smaller-fruited varieties should be grown in areas where summer temperatures go above 90°F. Always keep the plants moist when in flower; the least hint of dryness will cause the flowers to drop. As the leaves are shiny and the flowers attractive, peppers are ideal summer plants for the patio, deck or balcony. Because the plants are woody, when harvesting remove the fruit with pruning shears. Peppers take about 70 days to bear fruit and may be combined with other crops such as lettuce or carrots, which should be harvested before the peppers get too large.

RADISH

Radish is one of the very easiest crops to grow. If planted in loose soil, the radishes will be well formed. They germinate easily and, as they mature in a short time, should be used as a catch crop between other crops or as fillers with longer-maturing plants. Sow the seed directly in place and thin seedlings as necessary. The seeds may be arranged in rows near the edge of a container, with another crop in the center.

RHUBARB

This is a large plant which should be considered for container growing only if an area big enough is available to accommodate it. The crowns of the rhubarb are planted one to a large container. Keep the plants watered well and incorporate plenty of rotted compost in the soil. Feed generously with liquid fertilizer during the growing season and keep in the shade during the warmer months.

After three or four years, the plants should be lifted and divided (see page 118). In the early spring a small companion crop, such as sorrel, can be grown around the edge of the container. If the rhubarb should send up flower spikes, enjoy them as they are unusual and quite attractive. They should, however, be removed before seed is set as this weakens the plant. Tough, hardy and attractive, the rhubarb is a plant worthy of a place in your container garden.

SORREL

Sorrel is a low-growing perennial which will survive in a container through the harshest of winters. If planted in clumps in a shallow container it will develop and spread to occupy all available space. Keep the plants well watered and do not provide too much food. Pick the leaves just as they are mature and remove any flower heads which develop. Sorrel produces a lovely green foliage that will continue from year to year. Replacement is necessary only when plants have reached such an age that they stop producing large amounts of leaves. In areas where the summer temperatures are high, locate your sorrel plant in a shady spot.

SPINACH

This is a vegetable which will start to flower if the temperatures get too warm. Because of this tendency, it should be sown as soon as possible in the spring and may be started again in the fall when the temperatures have started to drop. Spinach is a very good container plant, especially if located in a shady area. Avoid placing near a wall where reflected heat can hasten the flowering process. There are bolt-resistant varieties which should be selected in areas where summer heat arrives early in the year. Keep well watered and, as the closely growing leaves hold moisture, try to give the water to the surface of the soil. Plants mature in about 50 days, so plan ahead for the succession of crops to follow in the container. A summer crop of peppers or eggplant and then carrots or lettuce, for example.

If there is a wet spring, mildew may be a problem. As a preventative, when you cut the leaves of the spinach, try to open the plant up a bit so there is room for air to circulate. The thicker leaves of the savoy-type spinach are somewhat more attractive than the smooth-leaf variety.

SQUASH

Since squash is a plant which requires a large amount of growing room, it should only be grown in pots to train on a trellis. There are bush types available but these are more successful out in the garden as they produce such a voluminous root that a container large enough to accommodate it would be impractical. If grown on a trellis, prune the vines to allow just two or three shoots to climb and tie them securely. Do not be disappointed at the apparent poor set of fruit at the start of the season. Keep the plant well fed and watered and be sure to provide it with full sun in the colder areas and light shade where the summers are hot. The container should be large enough to allow a minimum of 12 inches between the plants. Thus, a long narrow container of considerable depth is best. Remove the male flowers of the plant as it is best to avoid pollination of the fruit. These male flowers may be eaten in salad or fried as a side dish. As with other cucurbits, keep the fruit picked up to the minute, as it is best eaten when young and still tender.

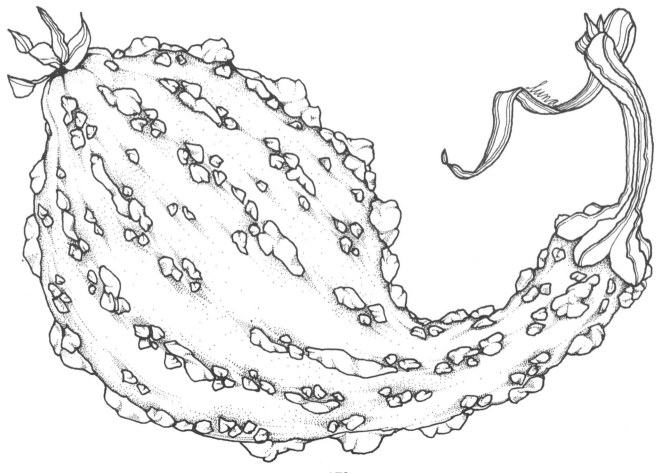

If the children of the house are interested in growing a pumpkin in a container, remove the rest of the vine after two or three fruits have set. This will allow for the production of larger fruit. Keep very well watered and feed with a liquid fertilizer. Watch for slugs under the pots and the leaves. Heavy watering attracts these pests.

SWEET POTATO

This vigorous grower should be planted in a very large container, only two or three plants to each. If only one plant is to be grown it must be put in a container which is at least 12 inches by 12 inches. The vines are most attractive and may be trained up a trellis or planted in a hanging container. The plants require a great deal of summer heat and, therefore, are grown most successfully in the hot areas of the country. They should be fed with a fertilizer which is low in nitrogen but high in phosphate and potash. Sweet potatoes are very easy to root from cuttings in a sandy soil mixture. When growing them, add a little more sand to the basic mix.

TOMATO

An ideal plant for container growing, the tomato is available in different sizes and shapes. There are a number of dwarf varieties on the market, for example, if you have a space problem. If you wish to use the plant for its ornamental as well as nutritional qualities, select one of the varieties which produce unusually shaped plants. Tomatoes should be planted as early as possible in the spring. Early setting out means a greater growing season and more fruit production. You may want to put a plastic tent over the container, which will protect the vines, and allow you to set out the plants several weeks earlier. Remember to use deep containers as the tomato must be planted at a considerable depth.

When first planted out, make sure not to overfertilize or overwater. This can lead to production of excessive foliage but little fruit. Keep the plants moist and restrict the number of side shoots which will appear to one or two. This allows for closer planting and, in so removing the leaves, greater exposure to sunlight. The removal of side shoots will, of course, bring earlier fruit and lower the total crop yield. Therefore, it would be wise to have two or three plantings several weeks apart.

In the cool of the morning, spray the tomato plants with cool water to keep the white fly in check and to aid in the setting of fruit. In exposed areas, protect the plants from hot dry winds which will cause a poor fruit set. If in doubt about the fruit set, hand pollinate by taking pollen from one flower on the end of a sable brush, soft cloth or rabbit's foot and dusting it onto the flowers of another plant. If staking is necessary, plant the stake at the back of the plant so it is out of sight. If you are growing the bush-type tomato, use a framework of wire netting, which should be placed in position when the plants are young so that the foliage will grow through the netting and hide the support.

HERB GARDENING IN CONTAINERS

Herbs are ideal plants for containers—large and small. The soil mix that would be best for the wide variety of herbs available is:

> Seven parts loam or good topsoil
> Three parts peat moss
> Two parts builders' sand

As the containers will need to be watered on a regular basis, I find it easiest to add a liquid fertilizer to the plants each time they are watered. If this procedure seems too time-consuming, add a slow release fertilizer to the soil mix.

Some herbs become invasive and are best grown in a container to keep their root systems in check. Mint is probably the best example of this. Mint plants will soon fill a container with their roots and seem to thrive the more the tops are cut back. Some herbs, like thyme, are very decorative and deserve an attractive container for their beauty alone.

Though many herbs are not deep rooting and shallow containers are usually sufficient for root spread, do not grow rosemary, sage, dill or any of the other taller herbs in shallow containers. While they might survive, remember that the larger the leaf surface of a plant, the taller the plant and the more moisture it requires. For this reason, tall and leafy herbs should be planted in deep containers where the greater quantity of soil will hold adequate moisture.

If you grow more than one herb in a container, make sure they do not crowd each other out. Mint, because it is such an avid spreader, should be grown alone. If you are growing taller herbs, use the space at the base of the plants for growing the shorter ones. Also, remember which herbs need to be sown from seed each year and do not grow a perennial in the same container as an annual.

As herbs are best when they are fresh and growing well, do not let them become too pot bound or the top growth will become weakened. Repot into larger containers each year or start another batch coming on.

The cultivation of individual herbs is fully described in another chapter of this book and these cultural requirements, in general, apply to containers as well. With a container, though, you can plant close to the edge and more herbs can be accommodated in a smaller area than would be possible in the open ground. Containers also require a closer attention to watering.

If your herbs are attacked by pests or disease, treat the entire surface of the container, including the underside. For this reason and to assure good drainage, I again recommend that containers be raised off the ground a few inches. This can easily be accomplished by placing a few flat stones or wedges of wood underneath. For permanent herb plantings, place the containers on a flat trolley with casters so they can be moved easily.

Crop Rotation

One of the problems that confronts the average home gardener is, "What shall I plant now?" There are many factors involved, the principal one being the weather. It is true that by using cold frames or cloches we can extend the season. We can also start vegetables indoors under lights and have plants ready to set out as soon as the weather permits, or we can purchase young plants from the nursery center. But even with these options, there is still the basic planning problem of assuring maximum use of the garden space available during each season.

You can plan an efficient use of your garden area by establishing your priorities and then following a simple formula. There are two givens: the number of days a crop must grow to bring it to harvest, and the length of the growing season. The growing season is defined as that period of time between the date of the last severe frost in the spring and the first killing frost in the fall. These dates vary from one geographical area to the next and can also vary from year to year in the same area. It is also true that some vegetables will stand a certain amount of frost. These should be planted so that they mature after the first frost, leaving a longer growing time for the more tender crops during the warm summer months.

The following plans are examples. They are based on four growing seasons: 365 days, which would apply to the warmer, generally frost-free areas; 280 days, for those areas where there is frost from the middle of November to mid-February; 200 days, where the frost comes in late October and the weather warms up again in March; and 120 days, where gardening is only possible from mid-May until the frost in late September.

Each row shown is in production for the length of the growing season being represented. By knowing the maturity time of each vegetable, a row can be planned with the sum of the maturing times of the vegetables planted equalling the length of the growing season.

It is likely that the vegetables I have chosen as examples will not be the same ones you will want to plant. Perhaps you do not like tomatoes but just love a vegetable I did not include. Just pick one or two vegetables with maturity times that total the tomato's.

If you are putting together your own garden plan, first compute the length of your growing season, then plan the rows accordingly. Don't forget the need to rotate the crops. Never follow a crop in a row with the same one; change them around. Remember, too, the maturity times for each vegetable will vary, depending on weather, gardening practices, variety planted, etc. Some lettuce varieties mature in 45 days, others in 75 days; also, the same lettuce variety will mature more quickly in the warmer months than at the end of the season. Another factor is that maturity times reflect that point when harvest begins and do not take into account the plants which can be harvested over several weeks, such as squash and tomato. Allow some time for cultivation of the ground between crops.

Crop Rotation Plan: 365-Day Growing Period

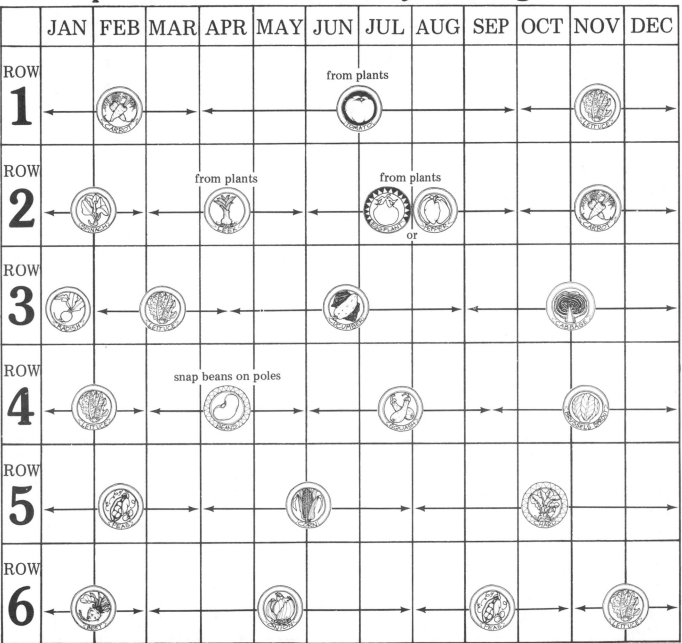

	JAN	FEB	MAR	APR	MAY	JUN	JUL	AUG	SEP	OCT	NOV	DEC
ROW 1		CARROT				TOMATO (from plants)					LETTUCE	
ROW 2	SPINACH			LEEK (from plants)			EGGPLANT (from plants) / PEPPER or				CARROT	
ROW 3	RADISH		LETTUCE			CUCUMBER				CABBAGE		
ROW 4	LETTUCE			BEANS (snap beans on poles)			SQUASH				BRUSSELS SPROUT	
ROW 5		PEAS				CORN				CHARD		
ROW 6	BEET				ONION				PEAS		LETTUCE	

Crop Rotation Plan: 280-Day Growing Period

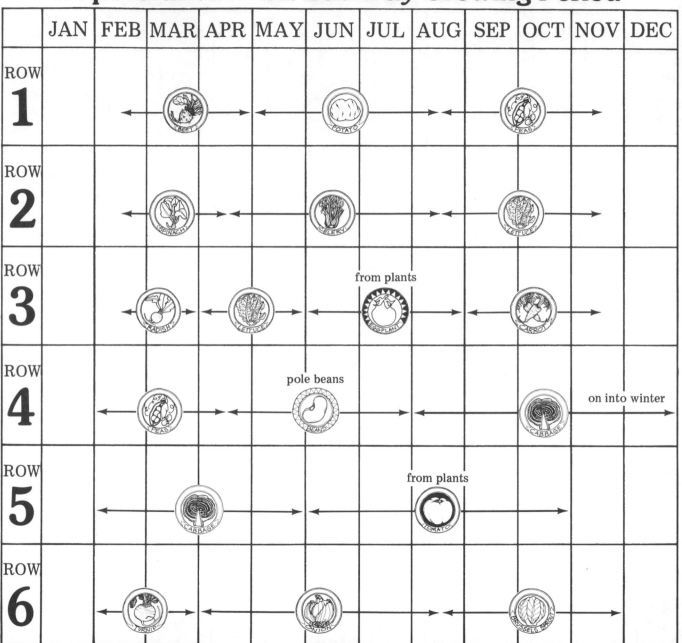

Crop Rotation Plan: 200-Day Growing Period

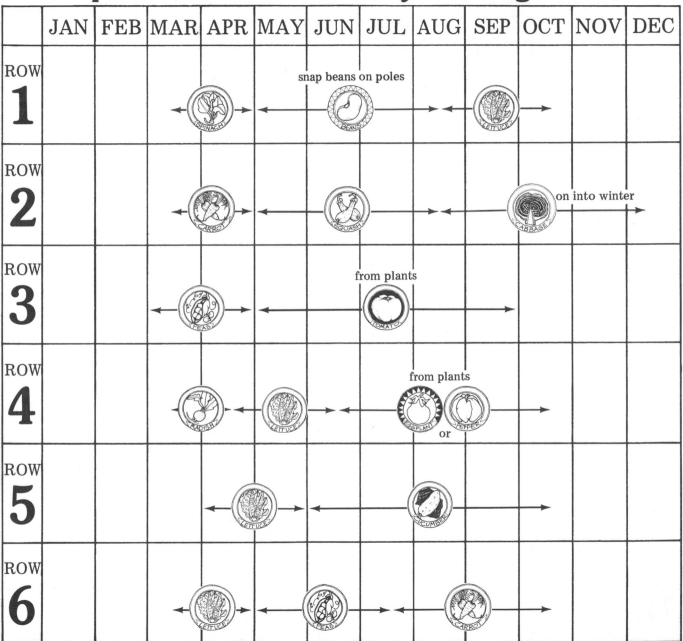

Crop Rotation Plan: 120-Day Growing Period

	JAN	FEB	MAR	APR	MAY	JUN	JUL	AUG	SEP	OCT	NOV	DEC
ROW 1						← SPINACH →		bush type ← BEANS →				
ROW 2						← LETTUCE →		from plants ← TOMATO →				
ROW 3						← PEAS →		from plants ← PEPPER →				
ROW 4						← RADISH		PARSNIP → on into winter →				
ROW 5						← CARROT →		from plants ← CUCUMBER →				
ROW 6						←	ONION	→ on into winter →				

Vegetable Varieties

There are many varieties of each vegetable available from many fine seed firms. The inclusion of a variety in this list is not meant to imply that it is better than one that is not listed. The list is a guide only, showing the range of harvest times possible and giving some aid in planning a garden using some of the most popular varieties.

The numbers in parentheses after each variety indicate the number of days till initial harvesting stage. Some vegetables, such as tomatoes or squash, will continue to yield over a long period of time. The vagaries of the weather and the planting time within a growing season will also affect the maturity time.

In some cases there are varieties of the same vegetable that vary several days in maturing time. The quicker-maturing varieties are not necessarily the ones to be preferred. It may simply be a case of a smaller-fruited plant, such as a cherry tomato, maturing more quickly than a larger-fruited one, such as a beefsteak tomato. Harvest times can only be averages, and the disparity between times for specific varieties and the "average" can be as much as two weeks or more.

The letter "p" after the days indicates time from setting out seedlings; "s" after the days indicates time from sowing seed.

Bean, bush: Spring Green (45s); Tendercrop (55s).

Bean, lima: Fordhook (75s); Jackson Wonder (65s).

Bean, pole: Kentucky Wonder (58s); Scarlet Runner (65s).

Beet: Ruby Queen (50s); Crosby Green Top (60s).

Broccoli: Green Comet (55p); Waltham (75p).

Brussels Sprout: Jade Cross (85p); Long Island Improved (90p).

Cabbage: Markey Victor (65p); All Seasons (85p); Savoy King (85p).

Carrot: Pioneer (67p); Royal Chantenay (70p).

Cauliflower: Super Snowball (55p); Snow Crown (50p).

Celery: Summer Pascal (100s); Clean Cut (125s).

Collard: Vates (75s); Georgia (80s).

Corn: Blitz (65s); Sundance (70s); Silver Queen (95s).

Cucumber: Gemini (60s); Sweet Slice (65s).

Leek: Conqueror (80p); Giant Musselburgh (90p).

Lettuce: Salad Bowl (45s); Parris Island Cos (75s).

Onion, bunching: White Lisbon (60p); Stuttgarter (100p); Yellow Sweet Spanish (120p).

Parsley: Banquet (75s).

Parsnip: All America (125s); Large Sugar (100s).

Pea: Sparkle (60s); Frosty (64s); Lincoln (67s).

Pepper: Calwonder (75p); Ace (68p).

Radish: Champion (28s); Cherry Belle (24s).

Spinach: Viking (45s); Bloomsdale Dark Green (48s).

Squash, summer: Eldorado (50s); Golden Girl (50s); Zucchini Elite (48s).

Squash, winter: Gold Nugget (85s); Emerald (85s).

Swiss Chard: Large White Rib (60s); Rhubarb Chard (60s).

Tomato: Moreton Hybrid (70p); Supersonic (78p); Beefeater (60p).

Tomato (for containers): Presto (60p); Small Fry (70p).

Turnip: Just Right (40s); Tokyo Market (50s).

First and Last Frost Dates

State	Average date of last frost	Average date of first frost	Days of growing season
ALABAMA			
Mobile	Feb 7	Dec 5	302
Auburn	Mar 29	Nov 7	224
Gadsden	Mar 31	Nov 2	216
ARIZONA			
Flagstaff	Jun 6	Sep 20	107
Prescott	May 13	Oct 7	147
Tucson	Mar 18	Nov 20	249
Phoenix	Feb 11	Dec 3	296
Yuma	Jan 4	Dec 25	356
ARKANSAS			
Fayetteville	Apr 3	Oct 24	204
Hope	Mar 25	Nov 4	224
Pine Bluff	Mar 26	Nov 5	224
CALIFORNIA			
San Diego	none	none	365
Santa Monica	Jan 8	Dec 27	353
Indio	Feb 5	Dec 4	301
Placerville	Apr 12	Nov 3	205
Chico	Mar 31	Nov 20	234
COLORADO			
Gr. Junction	Apr 20	Oct 10	173
Denver	May 10	Oct 5	148
CONNECTICUT			
Storrs	May 3	Oct 9	159
New Haven	Apr 15	Oct 23	191
Cornwall	May 6	Oct 10	154
Hartford	Apr 20	Oct 14	177
DELAWARE			
Milford	Apr 16	Oct 24	191
Dover	Apr 17	Oct 22	188
Newark	Apr 20	Oct 17	180
FLORIDA			
Tallahassee	Mar 20	Nov 20	245
Jacksonville	Feb 20	Nov 20	273
Orlando	Feb 15	Dec 15	303
Tampa	Jan 15	Dec 20	339
Miami	Frost occurs too irregularly to chart. Many years frost-free.		
GEORGIA			
Cornelia	Apr 15	Oct 19	187
Athens	Apr 12	Nov 3	205
Experiment	Mar 10	Nov 9	244
Valdosta	Mar 14	Nov 11	242
IDAHO			
Boise	Apr 28	Oct 12	167
Caldwell	May 17	Oct 5	141
Lewiston	Apr 5	Oct 25	203
Coeur d'Alene	May 12	Oct 14	155
ILLINOIS			
Rockford	May 7	Oct 11	157
Urbana	Apr 22	Oct 20	151
Griggsville	Apr 15	Oct 20	158
Anna	Apr 5	Nov 1	210
INDIANA			
Evansville	Apr 4	Oct 27	206
Indianapolis	Apr 16	Oct 19	186
South Bend	May 6	Oct 11	158
IOWA			
Mason City	Apr 25	Sep 25	153
Des Moines	May 10	Oct 10	153
KANSAS			
Concordia	Apr 14	Oct 24	193
Winfield	Apr 15	Oct 17	185
LOUISIANA			
Shreveport	Mar 6	Nov 12	251
Alexandria	Mar 11	Nov 13	247
New Orleans	Feb 18	Dec 5	290
MAINE			
Presque Isle	May 31	Sep 18	110
Orono	May 18	Sep 26	131
Portland	May 5	Oct 11	159

State	Average date of last frost	Average date of first frost	Days of growing season
MARYLAND			
Salisbury	Apr 20	Oct 20	183
Towson	Apr 15	Oct 22	190
Cumberland	May 1	Oct 10	163
MASSACHUSETTS			
Amherst	May 12	Sep 19	130
Concord	May 10	Oct 1	143
Fall River	Apr 22	Oct 23	184
MICHIGAN			
Traverse City	May 10	Oct 9	152
Grand Rapids	Apr 28	Oct 17	173
Lansing	May 6	Oct 8	155
St. Joe	Apr 25	Oct 22	180
Detroit	Apr 29	Oct 13	167
MINNESOTA			
Virginia	May 29	Sep 14	108
Rochester	May 11	Sep 27	139
St. Paul	Apr 24	Oct 8	167
Fergus Falls	May 11	Sep 24	136
MISSISSIPPI			
Biloxi	Feb 22	Nov 28	279
Crystal Springs	Mar 21	Nov 10	234
Tupelo	Mar 31	Oct 28	211
MISSOURI			
St. Joseph	Apr 11	Oct 14	186
Columbia	Apr 13	Oct 18	188
Springfield	Apr 13	Oct 20	190
MONTANA			
Moccasin	May 21	Sep 20	122
Bozeman	June 1	Sep 11	102
NEBRASKA			
Kearney	Apr 29	Oct 5	159
Omaha	Apr 14	Oct 16	186
Alliance	May 12	Sep 25	136
NEVADA			
Lovelock	May 13	Sep 23	133
Las Vegas	Apr 1	Nov 6	219

State	Average date of last frost	Average date of first frost	Days of growing season
NEW HAMPSHIRE			
Errol	Jun 1	Sep 5	96
Concord	May 11	Oct 1	143
NEW JERSEY			
Charlotteburg	May 12	Sep 26	137
New Brunswick	Apr 21	Oct 19	181
Vineland	Apr 21	Oct 20	182
Cape May	Apr 5	Nov 10	219
NEW MEXICO			
Albuquerque	Apr 14	Oct 26	195
Santa Fe	Apr 23	Oct 19	179

Note: wide variations in mountain areas

State	Average date of last frost	Average date of first frost	Days of growing season
NEW YORK			
Buffalo	Apr 28	Oct 22	177
Ithaca	May 4	Oct 9	158
Jamestown	May 14	Oct 6	145
New York City	Apr 11	Nov 6	209
Rochester	Apr 27	Oct 22	178
Long Island (av)	Apr 15	Nov 1	200
NORTH CAROLINA			
Wilmington	Mar 22	Nov 14	237
Pinehurst	Apr 7	Nov 1	208
Winston-Salem	Apr 14	Oct 24	193
NORTH DAKOTA			
Fargo	May 20	Sep 27	130
Devils Lake	May 25	Sep 15	113
OHIO			
Cleveland	Apr 16	Nov 4	202
Columbus	Apr 18	Oct 19	184
Cincinnati	Apr 9	Oct 23	197
OKLAHOMA			
Oklahoma City	Mar 29	Nov 4	220
Miami	Apr 7	Oct 26	202
OREGON			
Hood River	Apr 20	Oct 20	191
Medford	May 7	Oct 14	160
PENNSYLVANIA			
Philadelphia	Apr 21	Nov 10	185
Pittsburgh	May 1	Oct 1	153
Erie	May 1	Oct 11	163
Harrisburg	May 1	Oct 11	163

State	Average date of last frost	Average date of first frost	Days of growing season
RHODE ISLAND			
Bristol	Apr 17	Nov 25	222
Kingston	May 1	Oct 14	166
Providence	Apr 16	Oct 19	186
SOUTH CAROLINA			
Charleston	Feb 20	Dec 11	294
Columbia	Mar 17	Nov 18	246
Greenville	Mar 30	Nov 6	221
SOUTH DAKOTA			
West. S. Dak (av)	May 16	Sep 23	130
East. S. Dak (av)	May 12	Sep 29	140
TENNESSEE			
Milan	Apr 6	Oct 26	203
Cedar Hill	Apr 9	Oct 25	199
Knoxville	Apr 2	Oct 29	210
TEXAS			
Eagle Pass	Feb 27	Nov 26	272
Lubbock	Apr 9	Nov 2	207
Brownsville	Feb 15	Dec 10	298
Beaumont	Feb 28	Nov 23	268
Tyler	Mar 16	Nov 18	247
UTAH			
Salt Lake City	Apr 20	Oct 19	182
Logan	May 15	Oct 6	144
VERMONT			
Bennington	May 15	Oct 4	142
St. Johnsbury	May 22	Sep 25	126
Hanover	May 18	Sep 28	133
VIRGINIA			
Norfolk	Mar 25	Nov 16	236
Lynchburg	Apr 9	Oct 27	201
Wytheville	Apr 20	Oct 17	180
WASHINGTON			
Spokane	May 11	Oct 6	148
Yakima	Apr 24	Oct 16	175
Walla Walla	Apr 10	Nov 1	205
Seattle	Mar 15	Nov 20	250
Vancouver	Mar 26	Nov 10	229
WEST VIRGINIA			
Elkins	May 1	Oct 12	164
Martinsburg	Apr 29	Oct 16	170
Charleston	Apr 27	Oct 23	179
WISCONSIN			
Marinette	May 8	Oct 7	152
Milwaukee	Apr 26	Oct 18	178
Grantsburg	May 22	Sep 19	120
WYOMING			
Av. of lower elevations	May 18	Sep 20	125
Av. of higher elevations	Jun 10	Sep 5	87
BRITISH COLUMBIA			
Prince George	Jun 10	Aug 28	79
Vancouver	Mar 31	Oct 30	213
Victoria	Feb 28	Dec 9	284
MANITOBA			
Winnipeg	May 25	Sep 21	119
Churchill	Jun 22	Sep 12	82
SASKATCHEWAN			
Regina	May 27	Sep 12	108
NOVA SCOTIA			
Halifax	May 15	Oct 15	153
NEWFOUNDLAND			
St. John's	Jun 3	Oct 12	131
PRINCE EDWARD ISLAND			
Charlottestown	May 17	Oct 15	151
ALBERTA			
Calgary	May 28	Sep 9	104
Edmonton	May 14	Sep 14	123
QUEBEC			
Montreal	May 5	Oct 7	155
Quebec	May 18	Sep 18	123
ONTARIO			
Toronto	Apr 20	Oct 30	193
London	Apr 9	Oct 6	180
YUKON			
Dawson	May 26	Aug 27	93
NEW TERRITORIES			
Yellowknife	May 30	Sep 16	109

Ordering Seeds by Mail

There are two ways to obtain the seeds for your garden. You can order from a catalogue, send your money and receive your seed in the mail, or you can buy them at a local garden supply store. An advantage of catalogue ordering is that there is a better selection than is possible in most local stores. In addition, you will be able to take advantage of the newer varieties. However, before you try a new variety make sure that it is a definite improvement over what you have been growing. Check the number of days to maturity and the recommended distance between plants. These may be decisive factors for you.

A disadvantage of ordering seed is the aggravation caused when the ground has been prepared, the weather is perfect and the seed hasn't yet arrived. When ordering, you must allow ample time for the firm to process the order and get the seed to you. One sure advantage of buying your seed off a rack is that you have it right away and can sow at the most opportune moment.

Federal and state laws require that seed packets be dated and only fresh seed be offered on seed racks. A few older packs are sometimes left inadvertently, so always check the date on the packet to make sure the seeds are for the current season.

There are many firms that have excellent seed catalogues, some specializing in vegetables. The following is a list of some of them. Also included is a source for cloches.

Burgess Seed and Plant Company
Galesburg, Michigan 49053

W. Atlee Burpee
300 Park Avenue
Warminster, Pennsylvania 18991

Farmer Seed and Nursery Company
Faribault, Minnesota 55021
(Specializes in varieties suited
to short growing seasons.)

Henry Field Seed Company
Shenandoah, Iowa 51601

Joseph Harris, Inc.
Moreton Farm, Buffalo Road
Rochester, New York 14624

H. G. Hastings
P.O. Box 4088
Atlanta, Georgia 30302

J. E. Miller Nurseries
909A West Lake Road
Canadaigua, New York 14424

Jackson & Perkins
P.O. Box 217A
Medford, Oregon 97501

Earl May Seed Company
Shenandoah, Iowa 51603

George Park Seed Company
90 Cokesbury
Greenwood, South Carolina 29647

R. H. Shumway Seedsman
628 Cedar Street
Rockford, Illinois 61101

Sheridan Nurseries
1116 Winston Churchill Boulevard
Oakville, Ontario, Canada

Wyatt-Quarles Seed Company
P.O. Box 2131
Raleigh, North Carolina 27602
(Specializes in varieties
for the southern United States.)

For cloches:

Guard 'n Gro
61 Cromary Way
Inverness, California 94937

Index

Acid soil, 28, 44
Alkaline soil, 28, 44-45
Allium Cepa, 102-104
Allium Porrum, 95-97
Allium sativum, 140-142
Allium Schoenoprasum, 134-136
Anethum graveolens, 138-140
Aphids, 51
Apium graveolens, 80-82
Artemisia Dracunculus, 154-155
Artichoke, globe, 56-58
Artificial lighting, 41-43
Ashes, added to soil, 45
Asparagus, 58-60
Asparagus bean, 61
Asparagus officinalis, 58-60

Bacillus thuringiensis, 52
Basil, 132-134
Bean beetle, 52
Bean, 25, 28, 61-63
    in containers, 162-165
    pests of, 61-63
Beetles, 52

Beet, 44, 63-65
    in containers, 165
Bell pepper, 110
Beta vulgaris, 63-65
Beta vulgaris var. *Cicla*, 82-84
Brassica oleracea var. *acephala*, 85-87
Brassica oleracea var. *botrytis*, 66-70
Brassica oleracea var. *bullata gemmifera*, 70-72
Brassica oleracea var. *capitata*, 73-75
Brassica oleracea var. *italica*, 66-70
Brassica Napobrassica, 119-121
Brassica Rapa, 119-121
Broccoli, 66-70
    disease of, 54
Brussels sprout, 70-72
Bush bean, 61-63
    in containers, 162

Cabbage, 25, 28, 32, 44, 73-75
    disease of, 54
    pests of, 51, 52, 53
Cabbage looper, 52
Cabbage worms, 52

Capsicum frutescens, 109-111
Cardoon, 75-77
Carrot, 77-79
    in containers, 165
    pests of, 51
Cauliflower, 66-70
    in containers, 165
    disease of, 54
Cayenne pepper, 110
Celery, 25, 80-82
Chantenay, 78
Chard, 63, 82-84
    in containers, 165-166
Chile pepper, 110
Chinese cabbage, 75
Chive, 134-136
Clay soil, 25-26
Cloche, 36
Cocozelle, 127
Cold frame, 35
Collard, 85-87
Compost heap, 46-47
Container gardening, 159-176
Coriander, 136-138
Coriandrum sativum, 136-138

Corn, 87-89
  pests of, 52
Corn earworm, 52
Correns, 18
Crop rotation plans, 178-182
Cucumber, 34, 90-92
  in containers, 166
Cucumis sativus, 90-92
Cucurbita maxima, 125-127
Cucurbita moschata, 125-127
Cucurbita Pepo, 125-127
Cucurbita Pepo var. *Melopepo*, 125-127
Cultivation, 29-30
Cutworms, 52
Cynara Cardunculus, 75-77
Cynara scolymus, 56-58

Daucus Carota var. *sativa*, 77-79
De Vries, 18
Delichos sesquipedalis, 61
Digging, 29-30
Digging fork, 49
Dill, 138-140
  in containers, 175
Diseases, 53-54
Downy mildew, 54
Dutch hoe, 49

Earwigs, 53
Edible plant parts, 21
Eggplant, 92-94
  in containers, 166

Fertilizers, 44-45
Finger (carrot), 78
Flea beetle, 52
Food stored by plants, 20-21
French intensive method, 40
Frost date charts, 184-186

Garlic, 140-142
Globe artichoke, 56-58
Glycine hispida, 61
Green bean, 61
Green manuring, 25
Growing seasons for United States
  and Canada, 184-186

Herbs *see* specific herbs
Herbs in containers, 175-176
Hibiscus esculentus, 100-102
Hoe, 49
Hose, 49
Hot beds, 36

Insects, 51-53

"K," 45
Kohlrabi, 166

Lactuca sativa, 97-99
Leaf crops, 41, 44
Leaf miners, 52
Leafhoppers, 51
Leek, 25, 32, 95-97
Lettuce, 25, 44, 97-99
  in containers, 168
  pests of, 51
Lima bean, 61
Loam, 24, 26
Lycopersicon esculentum, 128-132

Majorana hortensis, 142-143
Malathion, 51, 52
Manzel wurzel, 63
Marjoram, 142-143
Measuring stick, 49
Mendel, Gregor, 17-18
"Mendel's factor," 18

Mentha piperita, 144
Mentha Puleglium, 144
Mentha viridis, 144-145
Mexican bean beetle, 52
Mint, 144-145
  in containers, 175
Molds, 53-54
Mulching, 38-39

"N," 44
Nantes, 78
Nasturtium officinale, 43
Napa cabbage, 75
Nitrogen, 44
Nutritional value of plants, 19

Ocimum Basilicum, 132-133
Okra, 100-102
Onion, 32, 102-104
  in containers, 166
Oregano, 146-147
Oriental radish, 116
Origanum vulgare, 146-147
Osmocote, 34, 35
Oxheart, 78

"P," 44
Parsley, 148-149
Parsnip, 104-106
Pastinaca sativa, 104
Pea pod, 107-109
Pea, 25, 28, 107-109
  in containers, 168-169
Peat, 26-28
Pennyroyal, 144
Peppermint, 144
Peppers, 32, 109-111
  in containers, 171
  pests of, 52

Pests, 51-53 *see also* specific vegetable
Petroselinum crispum, 148-149
pH, 28
Phaseolus limensis, 61
Phaseolus vulgaris, 61
Phosphates, 44-45
Phosphorus, 44-45
Photosynthesis, 12-14
Pisum sativum, 107-109
Pisum sativum var. *macrocarpum*,
    107-109
Pod pea, 107-109
Pole bean, 61-63
    in containers, 162-165
Potash, 45
Potato, 112-114
    pests of, 51, 53
Pricking out seedlings, 34

Radish, 114-116
    in containers, 171
Raised beds, 27, 37-38
Rake, 49
Raphanus sativus, 114-116
Red spider, 52
Reproduction process of plants, 16-18
Rheum Rhaponticum, 116-118
Rhubarb, 25, 116-118
    in containers, 171
Root crops, 21, 26, 32, 41, 44 *see also*
        specific vegetable
    pests of, 53
Rosmarinus officinalis, 150-151
Rosemary, 150-151
    in containers, 175
Rotenone, 52
Rumex Acetosa, 121-123
Rusts, 53-54
Rutabaga, 119-121

Sage, 152-153
    in containers, 175
Salvia officinalis, 152-153
    sandy soil, 26
Scarlet runner bean, 61
Seedbed, 32
Seed catalogues, 187
Seed sowing
    indoors, 32-36
    outdoors, 30-32
    under artificial lights, 42-43
Sevin, 52
Silt, 26
Single spit digging, 29
Slow release fertilizer, 45
Slugs, 53
Snails, 53
Snap bean, 61-63
Soil, 23-25
    clay, 25-26
    cultivation, 29-30
    loam, 24
    peat, 26-28
    pH level, 28
    sandy, 26
    silt, 26
    sterilizing, 32-33
Soil mixes
    for container gardening, 162
    for herb container gardening, 175
    for raised beds, 38
    for seed sowing, 33
    for seedlings, 34
Solanum Melongena var. *esculentum*,
    92-94
Solanum tuberosum, 112-114
Sorrel, 121-123
    in containers, 171-172
Soybean, 61
Spade, 47-49
Spinach, 123-125
    in containers, 172

Spinacia oleracea, 123-125
Squash, 34, 125-127
    pests of, 52
Sterilizing soil, 32-33
String bean, 61
Sugar beet, 63
Sulphur application, 28
Summer squash, 125-127
Sweet potato, 174
Swiss chard *see* Chard

Tarragon, 154-155
Thinning seedlings, 32
Thyme, 156-157
    in containers, 175
Thymus vulgaris, 156-157
Tomatoes, 34, 128-132
    in containers, 174-175
    pests of, 52
Tools, 47-51
Trenching, 29
Trowel, 49
Turnip, 28, 44, 119-121
    pests of, 53

Varieties, partial list of, 183
Verticillium wilt, 53
von Tschermak-Seysnegg, 18

Watercress, 43
Wax bean, 61
Welsh onion, 97
Western Pulp Pots, 160
White fly, 52
Winter squash, 125-127
Wireworm, 53

Zea Mays var. *rugosa*, 87-89
Zucchini, 127

JOHN E. BRYAN is presently Director of the Strybing Arboretum and Botanic Gardens in San Francisco's Golden Gate Park and garden columnist for the *San Francisco Chronicle*. His career as a horticulturist, however, spans two continents. Born in 1931 in England, he graduated from the Royal Botanic Garden in Edinburgh in 1955, and did post-graduate work at the Royal Horticultural Society Gardens, Wisley, at the Hague in Holland and in France from 1955 through 1958. Upon completing his studies, he managed the herbaceous and perennial nursery of Vilmorin in Paris. In 1961 he came to the United States and became sales manager of Jan de Graaff's Oregon Bulb Farms. John Bryan is also the author of *The Edible, Ornamental Garden*, first published by 101 Productions and subsequently published in England by Pitman Publishing and in Australia by Penguin. He is a contributor to Sunset's latest books on pruning and bulbs and was general consultant for the book on evergreens in the Time-Life *Encyclopedia of Gardening*. In April and May of 1976 he was invited to Malta by the Maltese government to advise and report on horticultural activities of the island.

CATHY GREENE studied at Chouniard Art Institute in Los Angeles and presently works as a freelance artist. She has also illustrated the *Fabulous Fiber Cookbook* for 101 Productions, garden books for Rodale Press and Simon and Schuster and articles for *Yard and Fruit Magazine*.